TAPPING INTO THE FORCE

by

ANN MILLER

and DR. MAXINE ASHER

HAMPTON ROADS
PUBLISHING COMPANY, INC.

Cover design by: Lori Wiley
Printed in the United States of America

Dedicated to My Mother

———— ♥ ————

CLARA MILLER

TABLE OF CONTENTS

OVERVIEW————————————— 9
FOREWORD————————————11
ACKNOWLEDGMENTS ——————13
BIOGRAPHICAL DATA
  ON AUTHOR ———————————15
PRELUDE ———————————————21
   I. BORN KNOWING (Part I)————27
     BORN KNOWING (Part II)————39
  II. ANCIENT VIBRATIONS —————51
  III. FAR MEMORY—————————61
  IV. SOULMATES ——————————71
  V. ATLANTIS — MYTH
     OR REALITY?————————— 79
  VI. PSYCHIC ARCHAEOLOGY——89
  VII. THE PSYCHIC WORLD ————— 97
VIII. CRYSTALS, GEMSTONES, AND
     THE CRYSTAL SKULL ———107
  IX. SEDONA — THE RED ROCK
     SHANGRI-LA —————————117
  X. DEVELOPING RIGHT BRAIN
     ENERGY————————————129
  XI. LOOK TO THE STARS ————139
  XII. UFO'S - FACT OR FICTION?——147
  XIII. GHOSTS AND APPARITIONS——159
  XIV. UNIVERSAL MIND —————169
  XV. OTHER REALMS OF THE
     PSYCHIC WORLD —————177
  XVI. TAPPING INTO THE FORCE ——187
EPILOGUE———————————191

"TAPPING INTO THE FORCE"
OVERVIEW

Tapping into the Force is a book which examines the serious side, and the thoughts and feelings, of entertainer Ann Miller, as she relates a lifetime involvement with the psychic and spiritual worlds. Miss Miller, known internationally for her exceptional musical abilities, fulfilled the visions of a Cherokee great-grandmother who predicted that one great-grandchild in the family would have her intuitive talents. Now Ann brings her "hidden" psychic life into the open, as she reveals the events of her mystical childhood, of a life filled with extrasensory experiences.

Since she often helps others with her psychic talents, this book offers suggestions to sensitive people interested in "tapping into the force." Ann believes that some individuals can train their minds in order to draw positive energy to themselves, and has outlined steps to bring this about.

From the Broadway stage to the pyramids of ancient Egypt, to the marketplaces of Tangier, Ann's interaction with psychic energies is related to the public for the first time, including a past-life regression, under hypnosis, with former U.C.L.A. psychologist, Dr. Thelma Moss. Ann cautions people to deal only with doctors in the field of hypnosis. She also advises people to choose psychics, clairvoyants, and astrologers with care, since the field of metaphysics is filled with quackery.

The book gives techniques of meditation that have worked for Ann, ways to channel knowledge, and principles of mind training. Since Ann's experiences are the central part of each chapter, the book is entertaining, and instructional.

The author feels that, in this "New Age" of developing higher consciousness, only the soundest advice should be given to the public about psychic subjects, since people's lives can be endangered through misinformation. She has chosen Dr. Maxine Asher, author and professor, to collaborate with her. Dr. Asher has carefully experimented with developing right brain centers over the past twenty-five years in the fields of metaphysics and education. Together the two writers are a fountain of information about psychic subjects, since both seek to give validity to a field filled with half-truths.

We are living in a time when anything is possible. Yet we must have a formula by which our greatest possibilities can be realized. *Tapping into the Force* will provide the catalyst by which people everywhere can safely begin to open up to new dimensions of reality.

Finally, the book will demonstrate how a Hollywood celebrity, firmly rooted to the physical world, has used her own extrasensory abilities to bring a new dimension to her own life, and to the lives of those around her.

FOREWORD

By Jess Stearn

I have known Ann Miller for a good many years. I found her to be, as many actresses are, wonderfully intuitive, even clairvoyant. And I knew it was only a matter of time before she chronicled her experiences in the metaphysical field. As the dancing star of one of my favorite motion pictures, the perennial "Easter Parade," even then Ann had psychic impressions of her dear friends and co-stars Fred Astaire and Judy Garland. These she kept close to herself until recently, when she decided it was time to put her adventures into the psychic between the pages of a book. It is a book well worth reading, for it is a simply told tale of a remarkable woman's remarkable experiences in a field all too often tarnished by extravagant claims from people trying to create a sensation.

Miss Miller was skeptical at first even of her own impressions and experiences. She challenged them as they occurred. No trained investigator or researcher could have been more dubious of what her eyes and mind were telling her. But in the end, as I also did after a while, she used her five senses to come to the realization that the implausible and the unknown were true, when validated by the same stringent yardstick we apply to all events — psychic or otherwise.

"I would have to be a fool," she thought, "not to believe in the psychic gift, however it transcended the powers of the logical mind, when a prediction or an impression of an unlikely nature, was confirmed with the passage of time."

As I had, Ann felt in her search that she was dealing with the riddle of life itself. For if people implausibly could predict the future and see the past, what did this do to our conception of free will? It made me realize that our free will lies in how we respond to events meant to happen. But it also meant, as she indicated, that there was a design to life. "And given the design, there was a designer from whom we could take comfort." Her book is indeed a labor of love.

ACKNOWLEDGMENTS

The author wishes to acknowledge the help and inspiration given by the following people:

Bill Cox
Frank Dorland
White Bear Fredericks
Marvin Arnold Luckerman
Aboul Magd Mahmoud
Kamal El Malakh
Ann Mitchell-Hedges
Dr. Thelma Moss
Hermes Pan
Bob Prestie
Jess Stearn
Brad Steiger
Adele Tinning
Dr. J. Manson Valentine
Gordon Wheeler
Debbie Zehnder

MISS ANN MILLER

Ann Miller has been tap dancing since her earliest childhood days. She was so talented that by age fourteen, she played Ginger Rogers' dancing partner in "Stage Door," which made her a star. Born Lucille Collier in Houston, Texas, Ann has starred in forty motion pictures, such as "You Can't Take It with You," "Easter Parade," "On the Town," and "Kiss Me Kate." On the stage she was an incredible success as "Mame" on Broadway (1939-40). More recently, she has been acclaimed for her performance with Mickey Rooney on Broadway in "Sugar Babies."

Miss Miller has recently been seen on television, starring in the two-hour version of "The Love Boat" and just did a straight acting stint on TV in "Out of This World." She frequently appears on TV interview shows, including Johnny Carson, David Letterman, Merv Griffin, and Joan Rivers.

Miss Miller's lifelong interest in the psychic and spiritual worlds has inspired her to write this book, which follows her other biography, *Miller's High Life*, published in 1972. Currently, she makes her home in Beverly Hills.

DR. MAXINE ASHER

Dr. Maxine Asher is a teacher, author, lecturer, and explorer. She led the 1973 expedition for the lost continent of Atlantis off the coast of Spain, which received international recognition. She holds a B.A. degree in Psychology from U.C.L.A., an M.A. in History from California State University, Northridge, and a Ph.D. in Education from Walden University.

Currently, Dr. Asher lectures on ancient history, archaeology, and right brain development. As director of the Ancient Mediterranean Research Association, Dr. Asher continues the ongoing investigation of Atlantis, her life's work. She lives in Los Angeles, California.

PRELUDE

O ctober 8, 1979, 8:00 p.m. It was Opening Night of "Sugar Babies" at the Mark Hellinger Theatre in New York City. You could feel the excitement in the air. The mostly black tie audience was filing in with the ladies in their furs, beautiful jewels, and expensive perfumes. The air crackled with electricity. I was standing backstage in the wings, looking out into the audience, and I could feel the energy and excitement coming from the masses of people. My palms became wet, my knees shook, and my mouth went dry.

Mickey Rooney came up to me in his baggy pants clown outfit and said, "Have fun, Annie, relax, that's what it's all about. Have fun." Fun! I thought about all the problems we had while creating this show. The costume designers, the producers, and the directors were quibbling and arguing. Our dancers worked so hard and long that they were in constant pain. Truly, the six-month road tour with this show was like having a baby. The birth was to be in New York City tonight. This Sugar Baby was about to be born at last; only the birth was to take place in front of 3,000 people. TV cameras rolled, newspaper critics took notes, and opening night ticket holders of the hottest show to come to Broadway in years, were waiting to witness this birth.

I went back to my dressing room and got into my opening number costume. My stomach was in knots as I stepped on my small rehearsal dance board to tap and warm up my feet. I was still feeling nervous and tense. I've been in the business long enough to know that what I was feeling was opening night jitters. I went to the stage and waited until I heard my musical introduction. The four male dancers rolled me onto the stage as I sat atop a big luggage cart. My opening number took place in front of a huge movable train. The spotlight hit me, and something clicked in my mind, as I turned on another vibration. A force field of energy took over my body. Gone were the shakes, the nerves, and the upset stomach. Out came the professional, singing and dancing her heart out. The applause was deafening, and the rest of the

21

evening is now history. "Sugar Babies" was a hit. We ran three years on Broadway, and four and a half years on the road tour of the United States and then on to London!

What the world did not know was what happened on that opening night during the second act. Mickey and I came out to do a medley of tunes written by my late friend, Jimmy McHugh. The ending song was "Sunny Side of the Street." I was supposed to grab a straw hat off the piano and then whip off my long black satin skirt, leaving me in my tuxedo jacket and black stockings with my hat in hand. As I started to go down to the front of the stage to join Mickey, I sensed or felt a presence with a force that was so strong it almost knocked the hat out of my hand. I felt as though something was taking over my body. An unseen power seemed to go through me and into me like an electric shock. I felt as though I was doing the number but something very strong was taking me over and controlling my movements. Mickey felt it also and gave me a strange look. My voice was so loud and clear that it seemed I never sang better in my life. We ended to thunderous applause and bow after bow. We came off stage like two steam engines. I ran toward my dressing room and one of my earrings fell off. I thought this odd since they had adhesive on the back to hold them in place while I danced. I bent to pick it up as it rolled away from me. On a piece of large scenery backstage, the letters J.U.D. were apparent in white tape. My earring kept rolling toward the lettering, and my eyes seemed riveted to the J.U.D. Then a voice said, "Annie, it's me, Judy." I jumped up in shock and looked around. No one was there.

In the meantime, a couple of stage hands came to move the scenery. They seemed annoyed that the large piece had been moved much farther away than necessary. As they pushed the heavy piece away from me, the letters J.U.D. became Judge, Courtroom Set. I stood there frozen for a moment, as my dresser tugged at my arm telling me I had to hurry. I rushed to my dressing room to change into my military costume for the finale with Mickey.

After the show, I said to him, "You will never believe this Mick, but Judy Garland was on that stage tonight with us." He looked at me with a kind of wonderment and quietly smiled. It seemed as though somehow he already knew. At one time Mickey had been very close to Judy Garland during their MGM days.

The following morning the reviews of our show came out. Some of the critics said, "Mickey Rooney and Ann Miller did a medley of songs together that was strongly reminiscent of him and the late Judy Garland."

After this incident occurred, I kept a picture of Judy on my dressing room wall all during the eight and a half years our show ran. My dresser always put her near my make-up table so that I could see her.

I had worked with Judy in the filming of "Easter Parade" at MGM. During this time a warm friendship developed between us. Mickey and Judy worked together on several movies and she adored him in life. Somehow I felt she approved of the enormous success Mickey and I had in this old valentine of a show called "Sugar Babies." It was the type of show business entertainment that she would have loved.

This is just an example of the kind of strange mystical things that have happened to me throughout my life.

Many years later, after "Sugar Babies" closed and I was back in California, the phone rang one morning and it was Mickey. He said, "You know, Annie, we were great working together. Many people think you are the best partner I've had since Judy Garland." Then, with wonderment on my face, and a quiet sense of knowing, it was my turn to smile.

CHAPTER I.

Born Knowing

PART I.

It is possible that there are human emanations of which we are ignorant. Do you remember how skeptical everyone was about electricity and invisible waves?

ALBERT EINSTEIN

In the early 1900s, it was very chic and amusing to be involved with mediums and psychics on the society circuit. In fact, it was "all the rage." Most of these psychics were charlatans and phonies. Little did anyone know that, in East Texas, my Cherokee Indian great-grandmother was probably one of the greatest psychics of them all. Where she lived, there were no telephones or cars. They only had wagons for transportation, or went on horseback. There was no electricity either, only kerosene lamps. The world of society was as far away from her world as Tibet is from our own. What was the "rage" in Paris, London, or New York, was never read or cared about in East Texas. The East Texans only worried about their farm reports and if it was going to rain or snow. They also fretted about whether or not they would get their Sears and Roebuck catalogue on time. Life was more peaceful and calm in those days but it was also hard and grueling.

Great-grandmother Lucinda was a medium and a natural clairvoyant. I never knew her but oh, how I wish I had. For years, my mother and grandmother told me so much about her. Mom was one of eleven children and they all knew and loved Grandma Lucinda. Of course, I hadn't been born yet.

The family lived in East Texas, in Nacogdoches County. Lucinda had a force field of energy around her that was so powerful, she could move a chair or a small table, merely by lifting her hand toward it, never touching it. She could stand a broom on its end and let it lean to one side and it stayed there until she dropped her hand, and then it would fall over. One of the many stories told to me about Lucinda was that one evening, about five o'clock, my mother Clara (the first-born child), Alice, my grandmother, and Lucinda, (her mother), were sitting on the porch. Lucinda looked up from the book she was reading and said, "Here comes my son, Henry, on his horse. He's slumped over the saddle. The horse is heading for our barn. Oh, dear God, Henry is dead." My mother and grandmother looked out and saw no one coming, but they were used to Lucinda making profound statements. They were uneasy and upset. An hour later, the horse went past the porch on the way to the barn and stood there waiting. Yes, great-grandmother Lucinda was right. It was my grandfather Henry slumped over on his horse. He was dead.

Lucinda became well known in the county for her psychic abilities and people came to her for advice and help. She was glad to help them but would never accept money, saying her abilities were a gift from God and to accept payment would offend Him. Before she passed over, she said to my grandmother Alice, "There will be one great-grandchild who will inherit some of my psychic gifts. Tell her to use them with caution and only in God's name." I was that great-grandchild.

Many people do not believe in the afterlife or in the spiritual world. If they are not "sensitives," you can never convince them about this subject and you shouldn't even try. Many people do not believe there is a God, or a Jesus, but they will admit there is a power of some kind greater than themselves. However, they usually will not accept anything they cannot touch, smell, see, or hear. In such cases, do not bother to discuss the subject of metaphysics — it's a waste of your time, and they wouldn't understand anyway. If you, however, are a "sensitive," and if you have experienced the phenomena of life after death, you will never doubt the existence of other dimensions again. For example, you cannot touch or feel radio waves or television waves, but you know they are out there because you receive the radio station or the picture from the television set. When you discuss psychic matters with non-sensitive people, they may think you are ready for the "funny farm" because they are incapable of having the experience themselves. So, if you are a "sensitive," just know you have been given a rare gift from that power "upstairs" that I refer to as God, and that you were also "born knowing."

When I was three years old, I had a most unusual experience. I was playing in my room when suddenly I heard someone say, "Lucille." A voice was repeating my name (my real name was Lucille Collier) over and over again.

"Lucille." I looked around but no one was there. I wondered who was talking to me.

"Lucille," the voice implored, "listen to me because I will be with you always." I had no idea who was speaking to me, but I knew that I should listen.

As I grew up, I learned to tune into the psychic and spiritual world whenever I needed help. It seemed as if I were two people. Lucille Collier, born in Houston, Texas, had unique psychic abilities. Ann Miller, singer, dancer, and actress, led the glamorous life of a film star.

In the early days, I kept my psychic ability under wraps for fear people would think I was a bit strange. Today, I am more open about my experiences since "channeling" is a familiar word in the "New Age." A psychic channel is a person who acts like a radio receiving set. There is a force field of energy, or electricity, around that person which creates a vibration between the psychic (or spiritual) world and the physical world.

I have always had psychic ability which greatly influenced my life. For example, when "Sugar Babies" ended in April 1986, after a record run of eight and one-half years, Mickey Rooney and I felt we had played it long enough. We were homesick and exhausted. Life on the road was great for making money but being away from home for so long was difficult. Mickey was tearful in his dressing room. He gave me a big hug and said, "Annie, it's been fun."

We said our good-byes and that night a big party was given by the producers for our company in a small cozy restaurant after the last show. Mickey left for Los Angeles for business reasons and did not attend, but I did. I wanted to say good-bye to a great and talented group of performers. I stood up and made my farewell speech. I said, "I predict I will be doing 'Sugar Babies' again. This is not the end of this show for me. However, I can't tell you where or when. I see myself still in it, 'tapping up a storm'." Everyone laughed and applauded.

Two years later, in April of 1988, my premonition about reappearing in the show came again. I always keep a red make-up kit for my theater dressing room that travels with me wherever I go. I had taken it to Sedona, Arizona when the show closed and unpacked all the cosmetics, putting it in a closet for safekeeping. It stayed there for two years. Before I left Sedona in April of 1988, I carefully packed it all up again to return to Los Angeles. Debbie, my secretary, asked, "Why are you doing this Annie?"

I said, "I'm going to be in 'Sugar Babies' again." She gave me a strange look. Then I got the telephone call and returned to Beverly Hills, California.

On May 23, 1988, Ernie Flatt, our director and choreographer, and Australian producer, David Martin, flew into Los Angeles to meet with me for lunch and talk to my agent about my going to London to do the show with Mickey Rooney. The deal was consummated and I prepared for the London opening in August of 1988.

In May 1988, I started rehearsing for "Sugar Babies" in the dance studio for the first time in two years. It was hard work at first, but I've been dancing since age six and it came back rather easily. After two months of rehearsing numbers from the show, three times a week, I was fit and in great shape for London. Shortly before leaving, I went shopping at a well known department store in Beverly Hills for some new clothes. I had just left the rehearsal hall and was wearing slacks, a blouse, and my loafers. I passed the dress department and looked at all the lovely "goodies." While walking along, I saw some shoes I admired and started toward them. All of a sudden, I slipped and fell on a newly-waxed and polished marble tile floor, coming down hard on my right knee, and plopping down on my left buttock.

I lay there, stunned, almost without breathing, and broke into a cold sweat. I heard my secretary Debbie say, "Oh God, Annie, are you all right?" I answered, "No, I'm not." Then a lady came over and tried to help me up. Somehow she got me to a chair, and I sat down, feeling dazed. Someone gave me a glass of water. I told them my knee was hurting badly, and so was my left buttock, so I preferred to sit a while longer. After a moment I thanked everyone, and managed to get up and onto the escalator to the third floor. While Deb tried on a skirt, I felt faint again and had to sit down in another chair. She glanced over and said, "Ann, you look ill; let's go home."

A plain-clothes detective came over to me and made out a report. He kept saying, "Shall I get an ambulance for you, Miss Miller?" I answered, "No. I'm a dancer, I'll make it to the car." When we got into the car I said, "Deb, I'm ruined. I'm hurt and there goes the show. There goes my big dream of appearing in London on the West End. Now they will replace me."

When I got home, I called the handsome young Australian producer, David Martin, in London. He was devastated. He asked, "Ann, how long will it take you to heal?" I said, "I don't know. I have to see a doctor. First, I'll go to a physical therapist to see if this will go away with treatment." As I hung up the phone and looked at my swollen knee, I knew I was in trouble. Then, my front pelvic bone began to hurt.

Finally, I went to my doctor and he asked me to have a bone scan. He reported the results: "Ann, I'm sorry to tell you this, but you have fractured your pelvic bone." I thought to myself, "Now I'm *really dead* for the show." When Mickey, who was in London, found out about my injury, he said that he wasn't going to wait around, and was going to fly home. They had to pay him extra money to keep him happy while I sat home, praying that God would heal me. I thought, "Why would a major department store wax a marble tile floor? How ridiculous!" Later, I learned that many people had fallen in the same department store, close to where I did.

I was disconsolate about holding up the show, but the producer called every week to see how I was and said that he would hold the show for me. He felt that the show belonged to me and to Mickey and to no one else. We had created the parts and played them for eight and a half years. I was very grateful to him, but I also learned that if we opened too late in the year, attendance would drop because everyone goes shopping during the Christmas holidays. I knew I had to get to London as soon as possible, but you can't put a pelvic bone into a cast. Healing was slow, yet, after six weeks I went back onto the dance floor and rehearsed. I did it slowly and very painfully at first, but finally I worked through the pain and regained my strength and endurance.

After I was feeling stronger, we packed all our clothes and Deb flew the dogs to Cincinnati to her aunt's home to be taken care of, as England would not allow dogs into the country. Then she flew back to Los Angeles and the next day we left on the plane for London. I had lost ten pounds and the director, Ernie Flatt, said I never looked or danced better. Mick agreed! That made me feel happy. Thus began our weeks of rehearsals and we were in great spirits. I knew the producer was worried that we were opening so late in the year instead of at the original time. His thoughts were focused on getting the tourist season business. I, too was worried.

On my arrival in London, and after a huge press reception and much fanfare, I felt truly elated. The press was very gracious and warm to Mickey and me. I felt thrilled but nervous. Would London like our show? Was it a bit bawdy? I was assured they all adored Benny Hill on TV and that our show was not as rowdy as his. I adored my new costumes, made for me in New York by Barbra Matera. I also found a wonderful hairdresser and a dresser. We had a great cast and wonderful dancers. All seemed to be going well.

Opening night finally came in September of 1988. The show was brilliant. All the important newspaper and theatrical dignitaries were there, along with prominent social people. Producers Andrew Lloyd Weber and Cameron MacIntosh and the King of Norway were among those present that night. It was thrilling. At last I was appearing on the West End stage. Ralph Allan, who wrote the show, flew in from New York. Director Ernie Flatt was exuberant, as other backers came as well. Our major investor, and my New York producer of "Sugar Babies," Terry Allen Kramer, and her husband, Irwin, came to the show. The opening night party was given at the lovely Ritz Hotel. As their guests, they entertained the Duke and Duchess of Marlboro, the Duke and Duchess of Kent, and other counts and countesses. My agent Tom Korman flew in with his wife, Pam. Mingling with all these important and scintillating people, my head was in a whirl. The reviews were wonderful for Mick and me and we knew we had a hit. That meant the show had "legs." In show business jargon, it meant it would run.

In November, two months later, while in my London Savoy apartment I said, "Deb, pack the bags, the show is closing." She looked at me as if I were ready for the funny farm. We had just opened in September, only two months earlier. She said "Annie, 'Sugar Babies' is a big hit and we have a great advance at the box office. What is wrong with you? When we left the states, we packed winter and summer clothes and planned to stay at least a year, if the British government would allow two American stars to remain that long."

"Please, Deb," I repeated, "start getting the suitcases up from downstairs. Call the porter now."

"Oh, Annie, relax. It's just another one of your "psychic" messages." Then she laughed and left the room.

"She'll be sorry she didn't believe me," I thought. "It's going to be so hard on us, packing everything in a hurry. The show will close suddenly and it's going to happen fast. My spirit world told me we'd have very little time."

All my life I'd wanted to come to London and visit all those places I'd dreamed about. Through John East, and a member of Parliament, Patrick McNair Wilson, Mickey and I were received by Prime Minister Margaret Thatcher in a private interview in her office, after we heard her speak in the House of Commons. She was a fabulous lady. She said, "Ann, please keep singing and dancing, because the world needs more music and laughter, and you and Mickey can do it all."

I also went with Jack Tinker, the noted London critic, to the State

32

Opening of Parliament in the Royal Gallery. Later, I met the Duchess of York at the Evening Standard Newspaper Awards. As if by magic, another friend, John Williams, had the Tower of London opened at 8:00 a.m., so I could have a private showing of the Crown Jewels, and an historic tour of the tower. Rooms were shown, not usually open to the public. During the American elections for the presidency, Ambassador and Mrs. Charles Price invited me to a midnight supper party to watch the election returns on TV.

I was caught up in a magical world of history and beauty. The very thought of leaving London made me cry. To top it all off, Mick and I were both nominated for a Lawrence Olivier Award, which is England's equivalent of our Tony Award. We also sang and danced for the Queen Mother and Princess Margaret at the Royal Variety Performance. We were presented to them in the lobby of the Palladium Theatre before the show, a first in the long history of this prestigious event. We gave them programs in white leather folders, which were hand embroidered. As a special honor I presented them with bouquets of beautiful flowers.

It was a thrilling time for us. Came Christmas and all of London was in a blaze of lights and music. Hordes of people were shopping and there was a flurry of excitement. But the West End Theatres were "hit hard," and most had half-full houses at this time, since people were concentrating on holiday preparations. Only one show — "The Phantom of the Opera" — was pulling in a full house.

Mickey became nervous over our attendance, as four big shows closed. He claimed that the crowds were so sparse because our theater, the Savoy, was on a side street, and off the main street of theaters. But the Savoy, an historic theatre, the first one ever to use electric lights on stage, was right next door to the fantastic Savoy Hotel. So many big shows had played the Savoy, I thought, surely this is not the main problem. David Martin, the producer, had so many concerns with the show, it made Mickey restless. The rest of the cast was also uneasy, so David finally came in, before a matinee, and announced that our show was closing. The cast was stunned.

It was a major blow, coming at Christmas time — everyone was so depressed. I gave a small Christmas party, and we all went out and bought each other gifts. I also gave a gift to everyone connected with the show. But it didn't help. The show was closing. I looked at all my beautiful new costumes, hanging like little orphans in my dressing room. "I'll be back someday," I told my dresser and hairdresser. "Plan on it. Keep my hair dryer, my coffee grinder and my electric fan, because I will return, just like MacArthur!" They all laughed. The British are the most polite and endearing people I have ever met. I would miss all my British fans and friends, but, somehow, someday, I knew I would be back.

Then the packing began. What a mess! There was the problem of packing all the clothes and Christmas presents. It had to be done fast in order to vacate my darling two-bedroom apartment at the Savoy, which was owned by American producer David Merrick. There was a big rush, because we had to leave on a certain date, or there would be another month's rent to pay to David Merrick. We were so rushed and we packed so fast, that my eyes crossed and Deb almost collapsed.

Just as the spirit world had warned me, it had happened. Deb and I were tired and sad as we watched the suitcases leave for the United States. I said, "Cheer up, let's go to St. Moritz, Switzerland and get some delayed Christmas spirit in the snow. We need the rest." Kevin Pauley, Debbie's boyfriend, who is Mickey Rooney's stage manager, was sad to see her leave.

After Debbie and I arrived in Switzerland, we took a breathtaking car ride from Zurich, checking into Andre Badrutts' Palace Hotel, still one of the great hotels of Europe. We had a beautiful two-bedroom suite, overlooking a lovely frozen lake. Gazing out, I clapped my hands with joy and said, "Come on, Deb, let's go buy some warm hats and go for a sleigh ride." I hired a sleigh with lots of sleigh bells, pulled by four white horses. We pranced over the ice-covered lake, up into the mountains and trees, where we saw the Swiss chalets. We bought cuckoo clocks and Swiss chocolate for our friends back home and gave each other watches. We went to Hanzelmans Cafe for hot chocolate and pastry and watched the skiers come in. Then we went up the funicula to the restaurant on the side of the mountain where we could see the skiers skiing down. We tried to be happy. After our final dinner at the Palace Hotel, which was served in the elegant grand dining room with waiters in white gloves, we said our reluctant good-byes. We tried so hard to be happy — but the "show had closed!"

When we returned to the States, after staying a month in my Beverly Hills home, I walked into Deb's room in the middle of the night and said, "We have to leave right away for Sedona, as one of my houses is going to be sold and I want to be there. Let's pack and take the dogs tomorrow." "Oh, Annie," she replied, "not another one of your 'psychic' messages. I'm worn out!" and she rolled over and went back to sleep. But we did pack the next day, leaving immediately for Arizona. Just as we arrived at my Sedona home, the phone was ringing. It was about 8 p.m. and my real estate agent said, "Hi! Congratulations, Annie, we've just sold one of your homes." I looked at Deb and broke out in a big smile.

In Sedona I had two houses. One I lived in, and the other I purchased for an investment. They had been on the market for three years, so I was delighted that one of them finally sold. I hoped the other house would sell soon so I could build my dream home, a Santa Fe Indian adobe.

Filled with excitement and anticipation, I ran into Deb's room and said, "I guess the old antenna is still working. This house just sold. Let's start packing." She looked at me in dismay. "Packing?" she said, "Oh, please, not more packing!" I laughed. She looked at me strangely and said, "O.K. Annie — you've done it again." Then we took the dogs out for a walk.

CHAPTER I.

Born Knowing

PART II.

I've been in the dancing business for many years. My beloved tap shoes, "Moe and Joe," are now forty years old. They are in the Smithsonian Institute, next to Irving Berlin's piano and Ginger Roger's dress that she wore in "Cheek to Cheek" with Fred Astaire. Now I have "new" tap shoes, called "Tip and Tap," which are twenty-five years old, and replaced a thirty-five-year-old pair, called "Frick and Frack." They never leave my side when I travel or go to the rehearsal studio. Dancers are strange creatures, with sensitivity and an acute sense of rhythm. They also have the ability to anticipate and forge ahead.

Understanding the psychic world always came naturally to me. However, people are often afraid of what they do not understand. They may also fear becoming a channel because of religious beliefs or personal prejudice against metaphysics. My abilities are natural but, through the years, I have come across some ideas to help sensitive people who want to "tune in" and begin the process of developing their own awareness.

Whenever I need help, I use my psychic telephone to communicate with the spirit world. I transmit the problem through thought, and receive the answer through sound or feeling. It's called clairaudience, or "inner voice." Sometimes, it comes through sight. I never formally studied psychic or spiritual subjects but, by my teenage years, I was so developed in this area that my keen intuition became a lifesaver.

When I was fourteen, I starred in a movie called "Radio City Revels." I told the RKO Studio that I was eighteen, fibbing about my age in order to keep my studio contract. The movie was a big lavish musical. I did a spectacular dance number called "Speak Your Heart," with a big chorus behind me. My costume was a very elaborate silver and black beaded gown. I was thrilled to be working with Milton Berle and others on this picture. Hermes Pan, the famous choreographer, who was known for his magnificent work with Fred Astaire and Ginger Rogers, staged the big production number. (During this movie, Hermes and I became dear and close friends. To this day our friendship continues to grow.) In his direction of the number, my entrance was to be made from under the sound stage, rising up to stage level in a small elevator. When the elevator stopped, I was to momentarily strike a pose and then break into my dance number. It was filmed on RKO's largest sound stage. In 1938, the sound stages had no air conditioning, only huge fans. It was extremely hot on the set, as the huge arc lights glared down at us from up above. There is a walkway, called the catwalk, suspended above and across the stage so that the lighting crew can get to the lights to manipulate them in lighting the performers and the set down below.

Later in the day, around 5 o'clock, due to the heat, I began to get weary and my feet were killing me. Yet, more important than that, my inner voice was nagging at me to stop and go to my dressing room and rest for a while. The director was anxious to get the final shot before 6 o'clock, as the production number had many dancers in it and was costing RKO a bundle. After six, they went into overtime for everyone. In spite of all that, my psychic since told me I had to go to my on-stage dressing room, money or no money. It was not a question of my feet hurting me,—it was this inner voice insisting that I stop dancing and leave the stage that very moment.

Francis Grant, Hermes Pan's assistant, talked to Hermes, who in turn talked to the director. He then yelled, "O.K. kids, Ann has to powder up, let's take a break." No sooner had I left the set when all the huge arc lights were turned off. A moment later a big crash shook the whole stage. One of the enormous arc lights had fallen in the exact spot where I had been standing.

My guardian angel must have been working overtime that night, and thank God I followed the guidance of that inner voice. I trusted the unseen and was rewarded with my life. All the dancers, Hermes, the director, and the crew, were extremely grateful that I had taken a break, for all that would have been left of me would have been two tap shoes in the middle of the floor.

Another example of my clairvoyance came a few days later. My mother, Clara, and I were at a cinema watching a movie. In the middle of the film, I announced, "We have to go home now."

She replied, "What's the matter Annie, aren't you feeling well?"

"No, Mom, that's not it. You see, there is a box of flowers dying on my doorstep and I want to save them." Sure enough, when we arrived home, there were flowers from an admirer at my door in a large box dying in the sun. I "saw" the whole picture in my mind. It's been this way all my life.

My psychic involvement seriously began in the 1940s at my home in Beverly Hills where I live today. Mother and I bought a game called the "Ouija Board." After dinner, we could hardly wait to go upstairs and watch this amazing device work. The planchette on the board went through the alphabet so fast, it spelled out words like a typewriter. There was a "Yes" and a "No" at each upper corner of the board as well. Eventually, the planchette moved so quickly over the letters, I had to get a third person to come and write everything down. Sometimes beautiful biblical messages came through and then there was a philosophical entity (a spirit presence from beyond), who said things like, "Things easily gotten are easily forgotten."

My friend Margaret Pereira used to come and watch. Soon she and I would take the board and work it at parties at her home. Rita Hayworth came to her parties between marriages, as well as Edgar and Frances Bergen, Evelyn Keyes, the actress, Tony Owens and his wife Donna Reed and, of course, Margaret's husband William Pereira, the famed architect. I remember once Edgar Bergen laughing at us while we worked the board. Just as the planchette went into a fast spin, it moved around and around, flying off the board and landing in Edgar's lap. He was shocked. He decided to ask the board a serious question. Apparently, the answer "shook him up" because he turned white when he heard it and didn't laugh any more.

Maggie and I became so good with the Ouija, we were invited to use it at other parties. We went to a big luncheon at the home of Dolly Green, whose family founded the Land and Rodeo Water Company, which is the site of Beverly Hills today. Dolly is a famed hostess and gives incredible dinner parties and luncheons. She heard that Margaret and I were playing the Ouija and asked a few ladies to come to lunch at her house to watch us work the board. She was amazed at the answer that came to a question she asked regarding her long-time romance. The board said she would never marry this man and he would pass over, which he did.

A friend, a well-known psychologist, asked if she could work the board with me one afternoon at my home. She was experimenting with LSD on her patients (with their permission), at that time. One of her patients was the noted film star, Cary Grant. She asked the board if LSD was harmful and the board answered, "Yes, yes, yes, it will leave a sediment on the nervous system which will eventually deteriorate the body and the brain." After that answer, she stopped using it and, of course, it has since been proven that LSD is a dangerous drug, to be used with caution.

Mother and I finally realized the Ouija was not just a toy but something to be reckoned with. We became quite wary of it and started using a card table for our questions and answers instead. To us, at the time, it was a mysterious game. We would turn down the lights and ask the good spirits to come and answer our questions. The table would rap once for "Yes" and twice for "No." Sometimes the table would do more than rap. It would shake violently, and once it fell over without either of us touching it. This game was no longer fun and began to frighten us just like the Ouija Board. What I didn't realize at the time was that I was a wide-open channel (like a radio receiving set). The force was coming through me. Finally, Mother and I no longer played these psychic games because the energies were so strong that other strange things began to happen in our home. For example, one night, I felt featherlike fingers touching my face. Then later I heard loud raps and noises in my room for weeks, so much so that I was unable to sleep. I learned that when the psychic mind is opened, it can summon up both positive and negative forces. To gain protection I had to pray and ask God for help. We had a priest come and bless the house. After that, I vowed never again to work with the Ouija, or the table, and never to play psychic "games" with the spirit world.

Many times since then I have observed people using the Ouija at parties where there may be psychics or sensitives in the group. These people often do not know they are psychics or open channels. When the board is used, dark forces can be unleashed that some individuals cannot handle. For that reason, it is a very dangerous game to play. The recent film, "Witch Board," a highly dramatized show about the Ouija Board, emphasized that fact. After seeing the film, and considering my own experiences, I felt I should warn people against the use of the spirit world as a diversion or entertainment.

I have been in touch with the spirit world from higher planes which I call the "good forces." My psychic ability has helped me through many distressing circumstances. For example, I had a premonition of disaster when I first walked into the huge open-air theater in St. Louis. I was in a show headed for Broadway, called "Anything Goes," which was opening at the St. Louis Municipal Opera House. One of the major backers of the show was Gloria Vanderbilt. It had a great cast, including Pat Paulson, Michael Callan, and Rodrick Cook. There was excitement on opening night. The place was packed. It was a revival of the old Cole Porter show, "Anything Goes," which is currently a hit in New York. In the middle of the show, as I finished the number "Friendship" with two of the stars, Pat Paulson and Mike Callan, the lights blacked out. As I turned to leave the stage, a big mechanical boom, or iron curtain, came thundering in and hit me in the back of my head. My vision became one-sided and I was in great pain. I could hear Michael Callan ask me, "Annie, are you hurt?"

"Yes," I answered.

When I was examined, the doctors told me I had what was called vertical vertigo, and a concussion of the inner ear, which also affected my vision. I had this condition for two years. During that time I couldn't walk without assistance, much less dance. I wanted desperately to dance again. So finally I went with my mother to a rehearsal hall to try and perform some steps. I prayed that I could return again to show business and the world I once knew. My faith was so strong that many months later I danced. My balance did return and I've danced ever since, with God's grace.

My belief in God has always been unswerving, yet today I think that God needs a great press agent! We need his guidance now more than ever, since the world has dropped to a very low level of spiritual consciousness. Recently I read that a six-year-old boy in Los Angeles stabbed his teacher in the back while she was grading papers because she kept him after school. Movie and TV violence, pornography, and drugs are part of the dark forces in the world today. Punk rock stimulates real life violence and gang wars are part of the problem as well. Yet, I know that the positive forces are gaining ground and eventually will win out. The Pope's visit to the United States in 1988 did a lot to rekindle people's faith.

As I read the papers and watch television, I realize there is still a long way to go toward restoring morality and sanity to our world but we are making spiritual progress. Even Russia has reinstated the Russian Orthodox Church and the Pope has visited there. In the "New Age," the ultimate goal of increasing psychic and spiritual awareness is to have better communication with your own beliefs.

One of the pioneers in the field of metaphysics is Shirley MacLaine. Through her writings, she has opened the way for people who were once afraid to discuss things of a mystical nature for fear of being considered strange. My former husband, oil man Arthur Cameron, told me privately before his death, that he hit the largest oil and gas field in his entire career due to an unusual circumstance. He awoke in the middle of the night and rolled out a map. He said that something guided his hand over this map and told him where he should drill. He

43

drilled in that spot and was fantastically successful. I believe his "find" was no accident. It was an inner voice or vision.

Debbie Zehnder, my secretary, came to me in an unusual way too. One night my mother looked over the railing of our staircase and said, "Annie, who is the little dark-eyed girl on the landing below?" I looked down and saw no one.

Mother said, "Well, she's standing there — I see her, and she's going to help you after I'm dead and gone." She was right. Debbie came from Cincinnati a year before Mother passed away and has been with me for eleven years as my secretary and assistant. She is of enormous help, and shares my interest in metaphysics, too.

I know that spiritual realms are very real but people have to open their minds to "tune in." Just because something cannot be seen, doesn't mean it isn't there. I always think about the story of the ice cube when I try to explain metaphysics to other people. If you melt the cube, it eventually becomes water vapor and disappears. The solid cube changed to another form, moving from the physical plane to another dimension of being.

Every activity is related to energy in some way. Dancers have great stamina but they always have sprained ankles or sore muscles. Even so, the show must go on — and it does. If I have an injury or muscle spasm, I go on stage in physical pain but I overcome it by using my power of mind or positive energy. When I had a torn Achilles' tendon, I left my show "Sugar Babies" for two months to recuperate in Santa Fe. While there I went to a tiny church in Chimayo, near Taos, New Mexico. This church was built around what used to be a small spring. The dry mud and sand, now in its place, is believed by the Indians to have curative powers. Crutches and canes hang on the walls from people who claim the spring has miraculously healed them. No matter how much mud and sand is removed, the level never goes down. Debbie and I filled two coffee cans with this mud and drove away. What a look the bellman in the lobby gave us when we tried to carry these large cans of mud and sand up to my suite at the hotel!

Back in the suite, we put a picture of Jesus on the fireplace and prayed together, rubbing the mud on my heel. We did this several times, but I was still in pain. Disheartened, I went to a doctor in Santa Fe.

He said to me, "Miss Miller, with your torn tendon I doubt if you will ever dance again."

I said, "Forgive me, doctor, but somehow I know I will." He looked at me skeptically but didn't say any more. Two months later I met with director Ernie Flatt in Florida. I told him I didn't think I could dance so soon after my injury. He said simply, "Try, Ann." I put on my tap shoes and said a silent prayer. I started to dance, slowly at first due to the pain and tightness of my muscles. Miraculously, in a week, I got back into the show. I believe my success in getting well was due to the power of mind energy, determination, and God's will.

Sometimes I can "see" events that lie ahead for other people. I met Henry Kissinger when I was his dinner partner at the home of Margaret and Bill Pereira. When I was in New York doing "Sugar Babies" in 1979, Henry and his charming wife Nancy came backstage to visit me. Henry loved show people, especially since the world of politics lacked the excitement and glamour of the movie world. That night, he seemed depressed as he spoke of his political future with the Carter Administration.

I told him, "Henry, you will be called upon again to come back to Washington to advise the President on the Middle East which is in such turmoil."

He laughed and said, "I doubt it. Not with this administration!"

"Yes, you will," I corrected him, "I can see it happening in my mind's eye." He smiled thoughtfully.

With the new administration, President Reagan did call him to Washington. He was to help the President guide us through the many problems with the Egyptian government, as well as those of Saudi Arabia and Jordan. When I heard the news, I sent him a wire saying, "Henry, remember I predicted you would be back in Washington to solve the affairs of the world? And you are." He sent back a wire on August 25, 1982, saying: "Dear Ann: Would you be my forecaster and press spokesman? Warm regards, Henry Kissinger."

In 1948, I began dating William V. O'Conner, Assistant Attorney General for the State of California. We dated on and off for twelve years. A divorced Catholic, he was tall, dark, and handsome. Every Easter Bill sent me two dozen red roses. Then suddenly he passed away from a heart attack and I was devastated. When he was alive, we would go to Palm Springs every Easter to spend the weekend at the home of Nat and Valerie Dumont. Nat is a prominent Democrat and we always had a wonderful time there.

After Bill passed away before Easter, Valerie called and said, "I know how sad you are Annie, being alone on Easter in Los Angeles. Why don't you come down and stay with us for the weekend?" I packed my bags immediately and made plans to fly down. When I arrived in Palm Springs, I stopped at a florist and bought a beautiful lily plant to give them. On Easter morning, as we sat in the living room and reminisced about Bill, I looked over at the lovely plant and said, "I can't help but remember the beautiful red roses I received from Bill every Easter holiday." Then I looked at the plant again and there, nestled between the green leaves, was one single red rose. I was stunned. We all stared at the plant and couldn't believe our eyes. How did the rose get there? The truth is I believe that Bill O'Conner wanted us all to know he was with us in spirit in another dimension.

Being Irish, Bill loved poetry and one of our favorite poems came to me at that moment. It was by Thomas Moore:

"Let fate do her worst
There are relics of joy,
Bright dreams of the past
You cannot destroy.
You may break, you may shatter
The Vase if you will,
But the scent of the roses
Will hang round it still."

I have had other strange psychic things happen in connection with people I cared a great deal about. Eleanor Powell and I were good friends. She was not only a great dancer, but most of all a great lady. She became a minister in the Church of Religious Science before she died. She always loved New York, where she started her career. When she heard I was in "Sugar Babies," Ellie wanted to come and see the show. By this time she had retired from her career. Eleanor Debus, Ellie's devoted secretary for many years, called and told me Ellie was very ill and she thought a trip to New York would be good for her. This was in 1982. When I heard the news of her illness, I invited them to spend the weekend in New York City and see the show as my guests. While planning the New York holiday, Eleanor Debus called again and said Ellie had passed away. I was shocked and so depressed over the news I didn't think I could do the show that night, as I had been such a great admirer of hers for so long. I sat down to make up in my hotel suite for the show and turned on the television. Suddenly, the TV went dark as there was a cable failure in the hotel. Then it came on again and there was Eleanor Powell, tapping her heart out in the "Pin Ball" number from "Sensations," a film Irving Stone had produced. After the number, the TV went out again and I said to Debbie, "Eleanor Powell came to New York after all. I felt she was there in the room with me to say goodbye." Eleanor died on February 11, 1982, a great star, never to be forgotten. The great dancer, Fred Astaire, was a friend of mine. After his death, Fred's lovely widow Robin told me that she sometimes feels his presence in her room when she is alone. The feeling is so strong, she can almost reach out and touch him. Robin senses that Fred wants her to know he is well and happy now in another dimension. He doesn't want her to be sad.

Through the years I have done considerable reading in the field of metaphysics. Albert Einstein is my "hero." In the 19th century, Max Planck, a German physicist, explained the theory behind time, place, and space in the universe. He laid the groundwork for the psychic movement by saying that there are particles in the universe that are timeless and do not abide by the rules of cause and effect. This concept is known as quantum physics, later restated by Albert Einstein. Einstein made metaphysics believable, and that is why I think so much of his great work in the field of physics.

Some years after Einstein, Professor Rhine at Duke University demonstrated, that people can "broadcast" messages across space to another person whose mind is tuned in to the same wavelength. This is known as ESP, extra-sensory perception. The other person receives the message at a subliminal level and acts on it. For example, Debbie almost always reads my mind. If I am in the rehearsal studio and have forgotten to bring my brush and comb, while I am pondering what to do, Debbie walks in with the items, not more than five minutes later. Another example of ESP is when I hear the phone ring and know in advance who is on the line, even before I pick it up. Sometimes I "feel" the death or illness of a close friend or family member before it actually happens, and sometimes I read people's minds before they speak. I also have premonitions which generally come true. These feelings come naturally to many sensitive people, not just to me.

We all have the ability to open up our "third eye." We are born with this psychic center. I am not scientifically oriented, but the "right brain" theory might explain how intuition works. Just as animals can sense a storm or an earthquake coming, sensitive people have the same ability — a sixth sense. Value your intuition and hunches. They might mean that your guardian angel is standing behind you and could save your life.

I believe it is necessary to have a strong faith to protect yourself from psychic energies which are not beneficial to you. I have that strong faith and it has sustained me through many experiences. I cannot give my belief system to others. Yet I think I have the ability to guide people toward the opening up of their own psychic awareness. In other words, "the force" is always there but people have to open up and receive it.

In the film "Star Wars" they said, "May the force be with you." I know it has always been with me and I wish you the same in your journey toward higher consciousness.

CHAPTER II.

Ancient Vibrations

"Though thou goest — thou comest again."

THE EGYPTIAN BOOK OF THE DEAD

I have traveled far and wide in my career. Yet, of all the countries in the world, ancient Egypt holds a strange fascination for me. Luxor, the modern name for Thebes, lies next to the Valley of the Kings and Queens. Just the sight, or mention of its name, causes me to cry with sadness or happiness. I'm not sure which. I even get tears in my eyes when I see a film that features Luxor, as in the movie "Sphinx." It is a riddle that I have never been able to solve. For some reason I was held back from visiting Luxor on three different occasions. Each time I caught an Egyptian virus and had to turn back. I was beginning to think someone had placed an old Egyptian curse on me. It seemed odd that I could never travel to Upper Egypt, the place of my dreams. Finally, on the fourth attempt, I made it.

My interest in Egypt caused me to visit the New York Museum when I was doing "Mame" on Broadway in 1969. I had been told by four psychics in four different countries that I was Queen Hatshepsut in a past lifetime. I was fascinated by the large statue of her in the museum, as the statue bore a close resemblance to me. Yet I was aware that other people had felt the same way about her as I did. Prior to that time, I had only seen pictures of the queen in history books.

As I stood in front of this statue and observed the remarkable resemblance between the queen and me, it seemed as if I knew the thoughts that she was thinking all those many years ago. Believing in reincarnation was one thing, but when I came face to face with who I was supposed to have been in another lifetime, the realization was startling! As I left the museum, I knew I had something to think about.

Each time I tried to go to Luxor, for some strange reason, I became very ill. The fourth time, when I joined Dr. Maxine Asher and her archaeological group I was more fortunate. Maxine and I had a lot in common — we were both interested in metaphysics and the ancient world. I felt this group would make it successfully to the Valley of the Kings and Queens, and I was right.

The group traveled to many ancient sites. In between touring, Maxine and I visited my dear friend, Kamal El Malakh, whom I knew previously from Cairo. Kamal had discovered a huge boat, called the

"Solar Boat," buried beside the Pyramid of Cheops on the Giza Plateau. (He uncovered a second one some time later.) The ancient Egyptians believed that the soul or "Ka" of the departed King could use the boat for transportation to his final heaven-bound resting place. It was almost two blocks long and had many oars for the King's slaves to pull the vessel safely to his new home. The boat had been reconstructed in a type of greenhouse building near the Cheops Pyramid and Maxine and I were among the few people invited to view it. No photos were permitted but, unknown to me, Maxine sneaked in a tiny Minolta camera and took a few.

Kamal was the editor of the Middle Eastern newspaper, *El Ahram*. Through his kindness and friendship, he arranged for us to visit the tomb of Queen Hatshepsut, which is normally closed to the public. He also made it possible for us to visit Queen Nefertiti's Tomb which has the most vivid colors of all left on the walls. This tomb was also closed to the public. Dr. Asher and I were thrilled to meet the Director of Antiquities, who became our guide to the tombs in Luxor. He took us into Hatshepsut's Tomb and I stood there shivering and seemed to go back in time, lapsing into a deep meditation. It was dank and cold and rubble was everywhere.

I said, "Hatshepsut was never buried in this tomb. The Priests put her body in her father's tomb, Thutmose the First."

The director stared at me, momentarily stunned, and said, "That is very strange of you to say that. We've just discovered five mummies in her father's tomb. We think one of them could be a woman but no one knows this except a small group of archaeologists." After a few moments of utter silence, we left Hatshepsut's tomb.

The Director of Antiquities took us to his home for a cold drink after the tour of the tomb. As I walked out through a patio, I felt a sharp sting on my ankle. I reached down to touch the area and realized I had been struck by a scorpion or small serpent of some kind. My leg swelled quickly and I became very ill. I was in such pain I was told by a doctor to go back to the States immediately. Finally, my friends got me on a plane, everyone was notified, and the doctors in Los Angeles were on standby for my arrival. For three weeks, I stayed in bed with a high fever, half out of my mind. I thought about the possibility that I had been the victim of an ancient curse or just plain bad luck. I will never know.

When I recovered, I continued to search for information about

Queen Hatshepsut, which was extremely difficult to find. One incident was particularly fascinating. According to the history books, Hatshepsut sent her men with ships to a far off country called, "Punt." Today some people think "Punt" is the modern country of Somalia in Africa. The Queen adored the perfumes of Myrrh and Jasmine. She wanted to raise her own Myrrh trees. Myrrh was not native to Egypt so she sent her ships out to find them in another land. Her beloved friend and architect, Sennemut, faithful to the end, undertook this long and arduous journey. After three years, he returned with the trees, which she planted at Deir El Bahri, her new temple designed by Sennemut.

Strangely enough, in my own life, I have collected hundreds of bottles of perfume. It seems I am constantly searching for a scent I cannot find. I know I must drive all the ladies crazy who work in the fragrance sections of the many department stores I frequent. I'm always hoping that the new scent will be the one I've been searching for, but it never is.

Archaeologists say Queen Hatshepsut may also have been the Queen of Sheba, which means that she visited King Solomon of the Bible in the tenth century B.C. and had a romance with him. This visit is recorded in Hebrew tradition and also in Arabic scriptures. If the four psychic readings in the past were correct, I must have had a wonderful past life as Sheba or Hatshepsut.

Due to my extreme reactions while in Egypt, and my avid interest in Queen Hatshepsut, Dr. Asher asked her friend, former U.C.L.A. psychologist Dr. Thelma Moss, to come over to my house and give me a past-life regression under hypnosis. Several people previously had tried to hypnotize me but were unsuccessful. Still, I was willing to try again. I had seen Dr. Moss give television personality Melody Rogers a hypnotic regression on TV. I was very impressed. It seemed so legitimate that I was eager to meet her.

Dr. Moss asked me to lie down on the sofa and urged me to relax deeply and close my eyes. Then she counted down slowly from one to ten, telling me I would locate an area of memory that would take me back to an important event. Here is what happened that day, as told to Dr. Asher in a letter from Dr. Moss:

"I asked Miss Miller who she was and she told me she ruled in Egypt as co-regent with her husband who was also her brother. She had a lover, but he was kept away from her by the Pharaoh. This broke her heart since she wanted to be with him. Miss Miller told me the Pharaoh hated her and wanted to be rid of her. He took away all her powers even though she sat to his right in a large golden chair in a great hall. She suspected he wanted to have her killed through the use of poison, so she had her food tasted to be sure it was all right. For protection, she kept a huge male lion, which she adored, next to her in the great hall. The lion not only protected her but was a companion as well. She told me she was dressed in a gown of sheer gold cloth.

"Then I asked her another question. I wanted to find out what she did in a typical day. She told me she slept in a low, narrow bed, all alone. (The Pharaoh did not sleep with her.) Breakfast was brought to her by her handmaiden named Tatu (or Tartu). She said her mother and sister came into the room while she had breakfast. I asked her what she was eating. First she said it was milk. I asked her if it was cow's milk and she said, No, camel's milk. It had honey in it but I gathered she didn't like it very well. She also ate a green fruit (possibly a fig) about two inches in diameter. I asked her what it was and she didn't know. I asked her if it was melon and she said she didn't know what melon was. Then Tatu helped her dress in a short dress above her knees. It was hot outside and the dress was of many colors of cotton.

"I said again, What did you do during the day? She said she went down to the ships with the ladies to buy material — blue and gold material from China. Then she went back to the palace to the royal dressmaker. The group was then scheduled to go on to see the architect who was finishing the temple at Thebes.

"Ann then told me she started each day in the Great Hall with the Pharaoh. Suddenly she burst into tears and was crying hysterically. I asked her what had happened. She said the Pharaoh had her sister and mother killed. She found their bodies in her bedroom with blood everywhere. She felt helpless and very sad. She hated her brother because of what he had done. She said he then poisoned her with wine and entombed her with her family and lover. She remembered that Nubian slaves were carrying her to her tomb while the priests were chanting. Tatu, and all the Queen's priests, as well as the bodies of her mother and sister, were thrown into the tomb together. The tomb was closed. The lion was by her side. Then the air began to diminish. Her beloved lion grew weaker and died. Then Ann said she blacked out slowly as she lay dying and gasping for breath. She felt as if she was separating from her body, floating through blackness. I asked her if there was more. She said she wanted revenge on her evil brother. It became difficult for her to speak. She seemed to go into a void.

"The next part of the session was unique. She said she saw a child playing in a great field of flowers which were of many colors. I asked, Who is this child?

"Mary — my name is Mary.

"Mary said, I'm visiting my mother, I've come to see my mother.

"I asked, Who is your mother?

"She answered, You are talking to her.

"I questioned Ann, Is there anybody else here? She kept saying she was floating and then said, You'll have to wait. I'm very tired. I am a very old soul. I have had many lifetimes."

That was the end of the regression. There were a few moments of quiet. Dr. Moss said I was shaking a lot and she also said I had chills during the session. After I slowly opened my eyes, all I could remember of the three hours was counting to the number two. When I was fully awake and calmed down, she questioned me. I told Dr. Moss about the death of my daughter Mary (in this life), and the brief and unhappy marriage I had to my first husband. It occurred to me that there may have been a parallel between the Pharaoh in my regression and my first husband. I also think the queen figure I saw may have been Queen Hatshepsut.

Dr. Moss indicated I was in a somnambulistic state which has never happened before to any of her subjects in a regression. This is a sort of complete hypnosis and she indicated it could happen again in future sessions.

I believe the regression cleared up many important things for me which I have worried about in this lifetime. First, I understand why Egypt makes me so sad and why I cry when I am in Luxor and other areas of that ancient land. Second, I have an obsession with lions — the stuffed variety. I have lions of marble everywhere in my house and, when I am working, my dressing room is filled with stuffed lions. I feel they are protection for me and fans send them from all over the world. Third, I am extremely claustrophobic and cannot stand elevators, small cars, or small dressing rooms. Finally, I need lots of oxygen when I'm working. I believe this could have come from the time I was enclosed in the tomb in Egypt.

One of the purposes of past-life regression is to clear away old patterns of energy in order to understand what is going on in the present. Dr. Thelma Moss was not only a good regression therapist, but she was quite legitimate in the work. Since she also has fine academic credentials, the session assured me of the validity of the psychic/hypnotic approach to past-life therapy. I was satisfied that the information she received from me under hypnosis was extremely accurate. It was also helpful in bringing new understandings to many long-standing problems.

My remembrances of the ancient world are not limited to Egypt. I am intensely interested in other cultures of antiquity, as well as unsolved mysteries like the lost continents of Atlantis and Lemuria, and the Bermuda Triangle. I see myself in many countries and have been told that in appearance, I could be Spanish or Moroccan. I am enamored of Spain and the Mediterranean area. Performing the flamenco comes naturally to me — as if I danced it in another lifetime. Perhaps I have danced down through the ages. Certain dances, like the Egyptian Nautch, or belly dancing, as the Americans call it, seem familiar to me in this lifetime.

I also love Mexico, Peru (particularly Machu Picchu), and the antiquities of both countries. I have always visualized the Egyptian masters during the Great Flood, traveling over the Bering Straits and teaching the ancient Indians how to build pyramids. After I formed my own views about this subject, I heard the same exchange of ideas discussed by archaeologists and metaphysicians, including the possibility that the ancients may have used levitation to move the pyramid blocks into place. The Russians have been experimenting with levitation and have had great success with moving small objects using mind energy. Recently, I observed paintings on the walls of the archaeological museum in Mexico City, which show the Egyptian masters teaching the Indians how to build their pyramids. Yet, this idea came to me psychically before archaeologists came to that conclusion.

I am strongly drawn to India. Psychically I sense that my past life there was quite sad. I'm not sure if I was a man or a woman but my intuition tells me I was poor, diseased, and blind. The country of India fascinates me and perhaps I will go there some day, which could bring back some sad past-life memories.

I also have a strong feeling for the Orient, specifically China. I love Oriental art and antiquities. In the late fifties, I had a lovely home done by the well-known decorator, Gladys Belzer, Loretta Young's mother. The decor was aesthetically very pleasing to me since it was filled with

Oriental antiques. I feel I had a past life in China and plan to go there to re-establish that connection.

The final incarnation that I can recall psychically is with the American Indians, which is probably why I've been drawn to the Sedona, Arizona area. Of course, I am part Cherokee, but that alone does not account for my strong interest in helping Native Americans.

At a recent charity party in Beverly Hills, I met Ted Danson of the TV series, "Cheers," and his charming wife. Ted is a great actor and has been very successful on this show. Yet when I see him on TV, or in films, he appears to me to be more the type to play an adventurer in a film like "Raiders of the Lost Ark." We introduced ourselves and he told me, "I've just finished building a Santa Fe adobe home in Los Angeles. I read where you are soon to build the same type of home in Sedona. I feel you love Sedona like I do. My family and I own land there. I was raised there as a child with the Hopi Tribe."

During our discussion, I found out that Ted was brought up among the Indian people. Now he wants to help the Indian children and is involved in a group called, "Futures for Children," which I am also interested in.

We are both interested in the ancient history of the Indian tribes. Ted feels as I do that the white man has never treated the American Indian fairly. After all, they were here long before we were. We are the intruders in their domain.

Ted and his wife will be coming to Sedona and we plan to have dinner together. Small world, isn't it? Two strangers meet in Hollywood and have so much in common.

CHAPTER III.

Far Memory

No atom of matter in the whole vastness of the universe is lost. How then can man's soul, which comprises the whole world in one idea, be lost?

THE TALMUD

The spirit world has always told me that a basic principle of reincarnation deals with the purification of the soul, which goes through seven different dimensions or planes of existence. The earth plane is a schoolroom where spiritual lessons must be learned. This is called Karma. After the soul is purified on the earth plane, it is reborn to the next higher plane of existence. Ultimately, after many incarnations, it reaches the seventh plane, where it is united with the God force. This is called "Nirvana." Thus, I believe we are only "in training" on earth, as we seek to find our ultimate oneness with God.

Reincarnation is not well accepted by Western civilization, but is a fact of life in India and parts of the East. I am interested in Indian religion but my love of the ancient world draws me to its reincarnation beliefs. The Egyptians prepared for life after death. The *Egyptian Book of the Dead* speaks of beautiful levels of life for the soul that has lived a just life on earth. The Greeks had the same belief.

Socrates wrote, "If the soul is really immortal, what care should be taken of her, not only in respect of that portion of time which is called life, but of eternity!"

All religions mention the possibility of life after death but none are specific about its details with the exception of the Hindu faith. The Catholic religion does not accept reincarnation although in the Middle Ages, St. Thomas Aquinas, a Catholic, wrote, "The soul exists independent of the body, and continues after the body dies, taking up a new spiritual body." In the book, *We Don't Die*, George Anderson, a good Roman Catholic and a psychic, supports the theory of reincarnation. He states that Catholicism has a great deal of psychic phenomena in it. Therefore the Church should acknowledge past lives as psychic phenomena and not as the work of the devil. In the Cabala (the mystical document of the Jewish people), reincarnation is discussed, yet the Mormon faith does not acknowledge the traditional concept of life after death on earth.

I believe deeply in the Bible, but I also believe in the theory of reincarnation since I have had many past-life flashbacks of my existence in earlier times. I call such experiences "far memory." These events have occurred so often, I know they are not accidents or figments of my imagination.

The Egyptians were so concerned about life after death that they placed food and personal objects into the tombs to accompany the deceased into the next dimension. According to Egyptian history, early people were very deeply concerned with death and an afterlife. They also pondered the meaning of consciousness, which they believed could travel into other dimensions of existence.

In most religions, the belief is that you do not incarnate but go directly to God after death. In some religions, if a person's soul isn't purified at the time of death, prayers are offered by the living until the soul becomes cleansed and ready to move on. Thus, in almost all cases, the church intervenes in human destiny by helping the soul pass over. One can see why religious leaders would not want the individual to actively embrace reincarnation theory. Such ideas might eliminate the need for formal religion.

One of the best explanations for life after life was stated in *The Secret Doctrine* by Madame Helene Blavatsky, a theologian whose work is now carried on by the Theosophical Society. Madame Blavatsky, who was also an anthropologist interested in the lost continent of Atlantis, explains the seven planes of existence, tracing the journey of the soul as it moves upward through eternity. More recently, a Stanford University professor, Dr. William Tiller, commented that beyond the material universe are universes containing more subtle kinds of matter.

In psychic readings given to me through the years, many sensitives have indicated that I am an "old soul," which means I will probably move on to my next plane of spiritual awareness after I die.

In India, there is an awareness of the different planes through which a soul travels. Hindus believe that all living things incarnate and have souls. In their caste system, if a person is in a lowly position in this lifetime, it is because he is working on soul purification. In other words, if he is crippled or maimed, he is repaying a karmic debt. Animals are also revered in India because of their place in the scheme of reincarnation. The Egyptians shared this belief and mummified their pets in the same fashion as their masters.

Sometimes we have experiences that can only be explained as past-life occurrences. For example, in "deja vu," where you feel you have been somewhere before, it is possible you have carried this "far memory" down from a previous lifetime. Dr. Asher expressed such feelings to me, explaining that when she was in Ireland, she was offered a map of Dublin. She declined to take the paper, saying she didn't need it.

"Why?" asked the desk clerk at Jury's Hotel, "Have you been here before?"

"No," she replied, "but I already know where all the streets are located." Past-life memory? It's a strong possibility.

How do you account for immediately "knowing" people you are introduced to for the first time? For example, sometimes I have an instant like or dislike for certain individuals I have just met. After I get to know them better, that first impression can change, yet I am usually not wrong in my initial feelings. "The soul knows," and what it tells me is frequently correct. "Far memory" also expresses itself in other ways. There are students who can recall historical events they have never read about before. They may even get "A's" in history exams without "cracking a book." When the teacher asks them about their knowledge of history, they may claim they simply knew.

Some people shun certain areas of the world, or avoid situations without an explanation. "Far memory" can dredge up fear from the subconscious that has no rational basis in fact. There are countries and places I have avoided traveling to in my lifetime. One of them is India. I cannot account for my avoidance of that country, since I am intensely interested in Indian history, culture, and religion.

Many great people have had reincarnation experiences. Thomas Edison was fascinated with the possibility of life after death and was building a machine to tap into the world beyond when he died. The psychologist Jung said that man's unconscious reached "god-knows-where." It is in the mind where discoveries are going to be made, he claimed. Physicist Fritjof Capra claimed that because of discoveries in quantum physics, we must drastically modify our basic concepts of reality. To me this means we must develop a higher, more spiritual consciousness in our world today.

Lee Iacocca, the famous industrialist, speaks of reincarnation in his book, *Talking Straight*. He says, "I know there's got to be something after this life is over...I can't imagine that throughout all eternity I'll never see anyone I love again, that my whole awareness will just be obliterated..."

One aspect of reincarnation theory that fascinates me is the explanation of premature and remarkable talent. A four-year-old Beethoven plays the piano like a professional; the eight-year-old Thomas Edison flunks out of school but starts inventing things. There are children, aged five and under, who exhibit talents worthy of an adult. I recently heard a ten-year-old girl playing a violin at the Kennedy Center Honors. She sounded like a Yehudi Menuhin or a Jascha Heifetz. Her name was Leila Josefowicz and she played so beautifully in Los Angeles, it took my breath away. Lalo Schifrin, the great composer who discovered her, talked with me that night. We both agreed that she was a prime subject for reincarnation theory because she played so perfectly and interpreted classical compositions so well. Usually these children lose interest as they grow older and the veil lifts, or the spirit leaves them. Then they go on with their normal lives.

The search for the Dalai Lama is based on the theory of reincarnation. In Tibet, in 1933, there was an extraordinary search for the child who would one day be the religious head of the Buddhist faith. After the death of the Dalai Lama, oracles were consulted and omens were interpreted in order to locate the person who would take over for the deceased ruler. Among other signs, they were told to look for a house with a roof of turquoise tiles.

In 1936, three years after the former Dalai Lama's death, a team of investigators discovered a boy, not quite two years old, in a house fitting the description, near the monastery of Kumbum. The investigating team visited the family without letting them know their purpose. When one of the Lamas saw the little boy, he asked him to sit on his lap. The child noticed a rosary around the neck of the visitor which had belonged to the Thirteenth Dalai Lama. The man said he would give it to him if the boy could guess who he was. The young child was able to do this and he also gave the name of two other holy men of the Buddhist religion. The child was tested a second time and passed the test. Finally, in 1939, he was transported to Lhasa where, "on the 14th day of the first month of the year of the Iron Dragon" (1940) he was placed on the Lion Throne. This procedure has been used by Buddhists for centuries to choose the Dalai Lama. It is believed that, when a small child passes certain tests, he is the incarnation of a previous Dalai Lama who has come back in this lifetime to complete his spiritual work.

I viewed a videotape of a similar story which astounded me. In Tibet, a four-year-old boy named Ossian Maclise, an American, who was on vacation in Nepal, asked his parents to leave him in a Tibetan monastery after their visit. He was very upset and told them he had once been the "High Lama" and wanted to stay at the monastery with his people. After the boy's father died, his mother moved closer to the monastery to be near him as he learned his spiritual lessons. He took instruction from a monk who said that, in a previous lifetime, Ossian *was* the "High Lama" and the monk's teacher. Now, in this lifetime the situation is reversed and the monk is teaching him. The boy is amazing. He explained on the video tape that he speaks both English and the language of Nepal. He told about his "dharma" or work that he had to do as a Buddhist priest to cleanse his soul. He pointed to a man in the street who was crippled and said that if that man did his "dharma" in this lifetime, then he would be a well man in the next lifetime. At age twelve, the boy was sent to a Buddhist university of advanced studies in a Far Eastern country where he is now working to increase his spiritual awareness.

A story from India tells about a two-year-old girl who asked her mother to take her to the next village so she could visit her husband and children. When they did, she knew every person by name, the names of the streets, and the husband who died some time before. This story is not unusual. There are dozens like it.

Certain sensitive people can draw to themselves memories from other times, both pleasant and unpleasant. As the soul incarnates in life after life, it sometimes takes with it the experiences of previous lifetimes. Like a tape recorder, the conscious mind may play the same tapes over and over again, which causes confusion and strange behavior in this lifetime. Often we repeat the same karmic patterns until they are brought out into the open by a past-life therapist or hypnotist.

I had a reading with Reverend Lucretia Allinson, who clears up past-life problems with her patients. She explains, "We work with the Akashic Record (sum total of knowledge in the universe) and take each person into regression to find the root cause for patterns of thinking today which cause fear, stress, and anxiety. Then we bring in the new patterns of success, and love, to replace the old fear and agony we have carried over from many other lifetimes." The tape recorder of the brain has to have its tape changed before new behavior can occur.

Reincarnation concerned me at first because I didn't want to feel that everything was predestined in my life. But I soon learned that within each lifetime, I did have choices. If I didn't want to do my spiritual work now, I could avoid it, but I would have to "face the music" in another lifetime to come. That is why I have not been concerned with my life when the going got rough. Intuitively, I knew that trials and tribulations were a blessing because they were placed in my path to raise my consciousness. Wealth and comfort are not always spiritual benefits unless the person who possesses them has already paid his karmic debt, and is a highly developed spiritual person with these valued possessions.

I believe reincarnation should not present a conflict for some people, since all religions deal with the question of immortality and man's relationship to God. Today, more and more medical doctors and psychologists are examining the possibility of reincarnation. One of the pioneers in this field is Dr. Ian Stevenson of the University of Virginia. His book *Twenty Cases Suggestive of Reincarnation* fascinated me, especially the following account, again taken from India.

Sukla was a girl born in March of 1954, in the village of Kampa, West Bengal. From the time she could talk, she kept using the word, "Minu." As she got older, she was asked who "Minu" was and she answered, "My daughter." Little by little, she began to also talk about her husband who lived with the daughter in the village of Bhatpara. She also mentioned another relative named Khetu who, it turned out, had a sister-in-law who died and left an infant child named "Minu" in 1948. When Sukla was five, she was taken to the house in Bhatpara where she was able to name individuals and objects with no difficulty. When she met her former husband and daughter, she became very emotional and yearned to be with them. The case was thoroughly investigated. Dozens of people were interviewed and geographical locations investigated. Apparently, Sukla had a previous life in Bhatpara since no other explanations could be given for her memories. Her relationship to her former husband and daughter, and her ability to know directions, places, and objects from memory were amazing!

Another case from the *Journal of the Association for Past Life Research* intrigued me, because it dealt with a memory from World War II. This past-life association has six scientists with Ph.D.'s on its board of directors and only deals with cases that can be substantiated.

Under hypnosis, a young woman described a previous life as a twelve-year-old girl killed in a Nazi gas chamber (though she had never even been close to such a situation). The therapist asked (under hypnosis),

"Where are you now?"

"We're in a line outside this building. I'm no longer with my mother."

"What exactly are you doing?" he said.

She answered, "I'm holding the hand of another woman."

"How do you feel?"

"Terrible," she cried.

"Are you crying?"

"No, I can't."

Suddenly she yelled, "I DON'T WANT TO GO IN THERE." Then she described the smell of the gas, and she choked and vomited, reliving her death. It was a terrifying regression but a realistic one. Although she had obviously cleared a painful memory through past-life therapy, there may have been more information locked in her subconscious if she really did live through the Nazi persecutions of World War II.

Reincarnation is not a religion, it is only a belief or a theory. The idea of reincarnation can be found in many religions and is universal. Reincarnation may clarify many unexplained events that occur throughout our lifetime. For that reason it is a significant idea.

Past-life experience affects sensitive people. My advice to someone researching this subject is to keep an open mind and study the theory yourself, especially if you believe you have had past- life experiences of "deja vu." Eventually you may consider the possibility that you have existed before and will be reborn again and again until you have fulfilled your karma.

CHAPTER IV.

Soulmates

If, in the twilight of memory
We should meet once more
We shall speak again together and
You shall sing to me a deeper song.

KAHLIL GIBRAN

To me, love is the most important foundation in my life. In the Bible, in the Book of Corinthians I, it says,
"Love knows no limit to its endurance
No end to its trust, no fading of its hope
It can outlast anything. It is, in fact,
The one thing that still stands when all else has fallen."
I believe this expresses the love that soulmates have for each other throughout eternity. You may be a king or a queen, a wealthy movie star or a president, but without real love you are a beggar. Mildred Cram wrote a book, *Forever,* which she autographed to me in Santa Barbara years ago. It was a beautiful love story about reincarnation and soulmates. MGM purchased her book in the 40's but hesitated to produce it because of the spiritually tender and fragile story of love and reincarnation. They felt the world was not quite ready yet to accept reincarnation theory. Even though they paid $250,000 for the book at that time, it still sits on the shelf waiting for the day when it will be produced. I hope I can eventually co-produce this beautiful story as a feature film since I believe the world is now ready to accept it in the coming "Age of Aquarius."

All my life, I've searched for a soulmate with whom I could share a deep spiritual bond. Perhaps I haven't found him yet because my own soul has not reached complete purification.

Soulmates are drawn to each other in many lifetimes and, when they meet in the physical plane, they have soul recognition. This means they have instant rapport and often a lifelong, loving relationship. A soulmate is someone we have not encountered before, but in whom instantly we recognize shared experiences in other lifetimes. When soulmates meet, they always "know" each other. They can feel the bond between them. When a soulmate meets his other half, and one of the soulmates has progressed enough in his spiritual development to deserve this meeting, he or she may be more spiritually

71

evolved than his mate. No matter. When they finally do meet, they will recognize each other even if they are married to other people, are of a different race, or even of the same sex. They will know each other. This is fate.

If a person is lucky enough to meet a soulmate in this lifetime, it is for the purpose of improving a karmic relationship with that person. Sometimes, we owe our soulmate a karmic debt and we pay that debt by performing good deeds for him or her. In other situations, the person owes us a debt and we reap the benefits of their kindness. We never meet someone accidentally. There is always a karmic purpose when soulmates are brought together in the earth plane.

The Greek philosopher Plato was the first to write about "Twin Souls." Plato discusses the idea at length in his "Dialogues." We find the same idea in many countries and cultures, generally in the mythology that people have handed down for centuries. Egypt had "Isis and Osiris," India had "Rama and Sita," and Greece had "Cupid and Psyche." Even the "yin-yang" (male-female) principle of the Orient, reflects twin spirits. When Eve was supposedly taken from Adam's rib in the Bible, this may have indicated she was really part of his own spirit. Soulmates yearn for each other throughout eternity in order to experience complete spiritual fulfillment. Elizabeth Taylor and Richard Burton may have been soulmates. The actor, Patrick Swayze, claims that he and his wife are soulmates. When a female-male relationship appears to be perfect, lasting for decades, the chances are it is a soulmate relationship.

There is no separation in spirit. When we lose a soulmate in death, he or she is always with us. Although soulmates experience different rates of spiritual progression throughout the planes of existence, they may also have a collective karmic debt to be fulfilled together. William the Conquerer loved his wife from the first moment he saw her. They worked on many projects together and also separately, in order to fulfill their individual destinies. Romeo and Juliet were soulmates. William Shakespeare repeated this idea again in "Julius Caesar," with Caesar's undying love for Cleopatra. Their life together had many pitfalls. Unfortunately, when Caesar was murdered, the pair were unable to complete their karmic bond. Jacob, in the Bible, had the same love for his wife Rachel. This is also true of Abelard and Heloise in the Middle Ages, whose rocky road of life did not destroy the spiritual bond they had together.

An interesting facet of soulmates is that they usually are quite tele-pathic with one another and often do not have to do much talking in the relationship. They simply know what the other person is thinking.

So many great people throughout history have written and spoken of soul relationships. The great composer, Richard Wagner, dreamed that mystery schools (like those in Egypt), would someday abound on the earth. Wagner also believed the intuitive road was the only way to discover truth, and that music, art, and meditation would help man penetrate the veil of the unknown. Other famous people who advo-cated spiritual bonding were Robert Schumann, Lord Byron, Eliza-beth and Robert Browning (who were twin spirits), Goethe, Mark Twain, Dante, and Rosetti. So you see a great love between twin spirits is not a foreign idea in the history of mankind.

Should one leave a spiritual relationship if there are problems between the two people in this lifetime? The answer is a resounding NO. It is critical to "work through" soul relationships, since harmony will result from the difficult encounter in the long run. If a person chooses not to work through the relationship now, eventually they will have to do it in another lifetime, if you believe in the reincarnation concept.

There have been many classic love affairs throughout time, un-doubtedly based on the twin spirit concept, due to the close relation-ship between the couples. Mark Twain spoke of his wife as his eternal soulmate, although these two partners acted as if they were mother and son. Nathaniel Hawthorne believed his marriage was made in heaven, but the greatest love story of all happened between Elizabeth Barrett and Robert Browning. What pair of lovers throughout the ages have not uttered the words the Brownings wrote so long ago? "How do I love thee? Let me count the ways..."Elizabeth was an invalid and married Robert against the wishes of her family. She then began to do her writing, often stating a belief in twin souls. Elizabeth and Robert worked together as collective spiritual entities while writing their poetry. This often happens when soulmates come together. Frequently, their life work is as important as the romantic aspect of their relation-ship. Ironically, the Brownings both loved the Mediterranean, writing poetry with Greek and Italian overtones. He adored her and she him. They were perfect examples of an eternal spiritual bond.

How do you know when you have found your soulmate? Aside from the things you have in common, there is a feeling, an "inner knowing," that will not go away no matter how hard you try to forget the other person. Once you have encountered your twin spirit you will yearn to be with that person and will want him or her to come to you in this lifetime, especially if circumstances prevent the two of you from being together. There can be terrible pain when the two are apart, because the separate soul entities together make up one complete soul. Very rarely will one person recognize the soul relationship while the other does not. This can only happen when one of the two partners has a higher awareness, based on previous karmic experiences. Plato said the body and mind of the two separate entities are one. (Since Plato was the most metaphysical of all Greek philosophers, his works on the subject of spiritual relationships are frequently quoted.)

Soulmates are usually best friends and working partners as well as lovers. They are the "be-all and end-all" to each other in every aspect of their relationship and are a perfect union, physically and spiritually.

You may wonder if the marriages of soulmates are always smooth. Usually, they are. The spiritual bond is so strong that it overcomes many differences between the pair. However, there are times when even soulmates experience disagreements. Yet, they can always reconcile, never permanently separating from each other because of their great love.

Occasionally, a soulmate or twin spirit will come to a person in the dream state, from another plane of existence. This happened to writer Charles Lamb who found the perfect woman only in his dreams. In addition, soulmates are not confined to male-female liaisons. I am heterosexual but I realize that homosexuals may also have the twin spirit relationship with a partner. There is a crossover in this instance, causing two males or two females to realize they are soulmates.

Sometimes fear occurs when a person has found his twin spirit. It is the fear of loss through death, the idea that one half of the soul is left alone again. We sometimes hear of one person dying and a mate taking his or her own life shortly afterward. There are also stories of one mate dying and the other making the transition almost immediately due to illness. Both these instances may occur because the two partners were soulmates and must remain together as one soul.

Edgar Cayce stated the right to believe in twin souls had to be earned. By that he meant that it could only occur when awareness was at a high level, and karmic debts had been paid in previous lifetimes. (His own wife, Gertrude, his soulmate, died only three months after he passed away in 1945.)

Most individuals have considerable work to do in the earth plane before they are ready for deep spiritual relationships. The soulmate relationship is a very special bond, only given to people who have fulfilled most of their karmic destiny, and are ready to grow in spirit with another, kindred soul.

CHAPTER V.

Atlantis — Myth or Reality?

The sea lies about us...
The continents themselves
dissolve and pass to the sea...

RACHEL LOUISE CARSON

In June, 1988, while Maxine and I were working on this book, we took a well-deserved break and drove down to the beach for an early dinner. As we sat watching the huge waves come crashing in and slowly rolling back out, I noticed a gold chain around Maxine's throat with a medallion made in three spirals, all wrought in gold,

I said, "Tell me about your necklace. It is most unusual. Does it have some mystical meaning for you?" She put her hand up to touch it lovingly and answered, "It is the most important piece of jewelry I've ever worn. These three spirals are believed to be the markings left in caves all over the Mediterranean when the Great Flood came and destroyed Atlantis in 9600 B.C."

"But why three spirals?" I asked.

"For one thing, the Greek philosopher Plato said Atlantis was a spiral city with concentric circles of land and water, and a temple in the middle. The triple spiral also represents man in his most complete form. One spiral signifies our physical being, the second our psychic self, and the third our spiritual soul."

"How do you know this? I've never seen it written anywhere," I asked her.

Maxine said, "Many people have tried to interpret the three spirals. The best book on the subject is called, *The Mystic Spiral*. The spiral is a universal symbol. It actually represents timelessness or eternity in its simplest form."

By now I was very intrigued.

I asked, "Where have you found these spirals, Maxine?"

She said, "I first observed them in the caves of the Guanche Indians on the Canary Islands after a strange clairvoyant dream. They were triple spirals, discovered on the island of La Palma, the outermost of the Canary Chain. The very next day, I photographed them in the caves. After that, I viewed identical ones in Ireland at the Caves of Newgrange, and later on the island of Malta. These areas are all connected to places where Atlantean survivors probably went after the

Great Flood."

I said, "I've always been interested in stories of the lost continent of Atlantis but, like other people, I was skeptical about its existence, since I had never seen any physical proof. Now you are sitting in front of me insisting that you, and others, have actually found remains of Atlantis." It was a fascinating thought and I wanted to hear more.

After dinner we drove back to my home to continue working on the book. I offered to run a movie for Maxine called "Atlantis," that friends of mine had produced. Theodore Rubanis, and his wife at the time, Lady Sarah Spencer Churchill, gave me a copy. It is a wonderful movie about the rise and fall of Atlantis. At the end of the film, it shows the Great Flood and all the volcanic eruptions, along with a huge pyramid collapsing into the sea. People were screaming hysterically and battling each other to get into boats and ships for evacuation. After the movie was over, Maxine said, "You know Annie, one of the best novels ever written about Atlantis was written by Taylor Caldwell when she was only twelve years old. It is called *The Romance of Atlantis*, and was released after she became a best-selling author. The book was so worldly wise her parents and teachers were shocked. Jess Stearn worked with Taylor to re-edit and publish the book. It demonstrates she may have lived on Atlantis in another lifetime. Perhaps that's why she had such total recall or far memory."

Maxine continued, "In 1982, I received a call from Taylor Caldwell's husband, Bob Prestie. Taylor had insisted I come for lunch. I was thrilled. When I arrived, I found she was both deaf and mute, a condition resulting from an earlier stroke. Her impairment was a shock to me, but with Bob's help she asked me questions about Atlantis. I believe Taylor had a great interest in my Atlantis work because she seemed very emotional about the visit."

I asked, "Maxine, can you give me some scientific evidence for the existence of Atlantis?"

"Yes, but first I must tell you that devoted family and friends have spent over $200,000 since 1958, helping me search for Atlantis. It destroyed three of my marriages and almost brought about my arrest in Spain." I was shocked at what Maxine was telling me. What a nightmare she must have experienced while pursuing her dream!

"And now, are you still searching for the lost continent after all you've been through?"

"Yes, Ann, we've only just begun. I believe Atlantis is the most wonderful subject in the world. It covers fourteen different subjects, including history, geology, geography, mythology, and the Bible."

"How did we first learn about Atlantis?" I asked her.

"The first written record of the lost continent comes from the Greek philosopher Plato. In his *Dialogues*, the "Timaeus" and "Critias," he claimed that Atlantis lay beyond the Gates of Hercules, one of which is Gibraltar and the other Tangier. He said the Atlanteans were a peaceful people who created a remarkable civilization. Later, Edgar Cayce and other psychics said the Atlanteans used mind power as a source of energy."

"Mind power — how did they use it?" I asked her.

"Cayce said the people communicated telepathically and also moved objects with the power of mind. They even sent and received messages using crystals. Unfortunately, their civilization was short-lived. In the last days, about 9600 B.C., the Cayce readings say that the Atlanteans misused this energy and brought about the end of their culture."

"What other reasons were there for the destruction of Atlantis?" I asked.

"Plato said Atlantis sank in a day and a night. We're not sure if the destruction occurred that quickly but we do know there was a world-wide flood in 9600 B.C. which caused the waters to rise all across the Atlantic Ocean. They reached a height of 200 feet, a figure verified by an oceanographer friend of mine at Scripps Institute of Oceanography and Dr. Cesare Emiliani of the University of Miami. He wrote about the flood in *Science Magazine* in 1976, mentioning Plato and Atlantis. Recently, in 1989, Danish scientists, working at the poles, stated there was a sudden ice melt about 10,000 B.C., that caused a great flood."

"Where do you think Atlantis is today?"

"I believe the remnants of the city, as described by Plato, lie underwater near Gibraltar. This city was once part of a larger land mass that spanned the entire Atlantic Ocean.

"It sounds like Atlantis was everywhere," I said.

"Not everywhere, only in the Atlantic. Our diving group observed some remnants of Atlantis in Spain in 1973, twenty miles north of Gibraltar, at a site called Barbeta, near Cadiz. The area was close to Plato's location for the lost continent.

"That's where you had so much trouble, isn't it?"

"Yes, accidentally we got mixed up in an intended Communist

81

takeover of Spain. This event was quite a shock to me. We were searching, with official Spanish permits from the Department of Belles Artes in Madrid. Unfortunately, our divers were too close to the U.S. Naval Base at Rota, where the waters are mined and filled with uranium."

"Hadn't you worked in Spain before?" I asked her.

"Yes, I conducted research there for twenty years with no problems at all. The Spanish people I worked with were wonderful to me. I speak their language and so does Dr. Julian Nava, former U.S. Ambassador to Mexico, who led the search with me. By the way, the Great Flood may have been the Flood of Noah. The ark probably was real, landing on Mt. Ararat as the Bible said. Four hundred years later, when the waters receded, Jericho was founded in 9200 B.C., just a short time after Atlantis sank."

"Well, who were the Atlanteans? How did they get to their island in the first place?" I asked.

"There are many theories. Some people say they came from outer space. Others believe they came from Lemuria, an older civilization in the Pacific that was destroyed before Atlantis. Some scientists think Atlantean survivors may have become Cro-Magnon man, who was so much more civilized than his contemporary, Neanderthal. Cro-Magnon fled to the mountains of northern Spain about 12,000 B.C. and no one knows where they originated. That might make the present day Basques the descendants of Atlantis."

"What about Spain? Why have you concentrated your research there?" I asked, a bit puzzled.

"Well, if it is true that Cro-Magnon fled from sinking Atlantis into Spain, then perhaps other people who occupied Spain at a later date also came from Atlantis, like the Celts and the Hebrews."

"That makes sense," I told her, "But it's getting late. Let's finish this conversation tomorrow night." Now I was "hooked" on the subject and had to hear as much as I could.

The next night I was like a child in a candy store. I had a list of questions for Maxine a mile long.

"Maxine, whenever I think about Atlantis, psychically, I feel it was in the Bermuda Triangle area, not Spain."

"You are not alone in your feelings, Annie. The great Edgar Cayce said the last piece of Atlantis, called Poseidia, was in that location."

"Is there any physical proof about Atlantis being near the Bermuda

Triangle? Have there been any expeditions?"

"Lots of them, but the most convincing work was done by J. Manson Valentine, Ph.D., who discovered the underwater temple blocks at Bimini Island in the Bahamas in 1968 with a grant from the Edgar Cayce Foundation. The blocks, called the "Bimini Road," are manmade and run for miles under the ocean. They date to about 9000 B.C."

"I'm impressed. Is there other proof?"

"Other expeditions were conducted at Bimini over the years by Professor David Zink of Lamar University and writer Peter Tompkins. They all agreed with Dr. Valentine that the blocks were manmade. The best work, however, has been done by the Russians."

"The Russians — where did they search?"

"At the Vema Fault near the Azores and at the Ampere Seapoint near Portugal. They found an entire underwater city, 600 feet down, similar to the ruins our divers discovered near Gibraltar, only we were not as deep. They used a two-man sub for their work."

"Who survived the Atlantis disaster, Maxine — did many people make it?"

"About one percent, we think. The great cataclysmic scientist, Dr. Immanuel Velikovsky, suggested this figure."

"What in the world is a cataclysmic scientist, Maxine?"

"That's simple — it's a person who studies world disasters. You see, land and water are always in motion. The earth goes through periods of upheaval when earthquakes, tidal waves, and even planetary changes cause almost total destruction. There are even shifts in the poles. Tropical vegetation has been found in the mouths of ancient mammoths at the North Pole!"

"Then the people who fear the California earthquake might have experienced a similar disaster in another lifetime?"

"Exactly — and the memory of those catastrophes may still be with them. The upheavals will reoccur. No one knows when, but we guess it will be before the end of this century. That may be why there is so little written evidence or artifacts from Atlantis. Too much was lost or destroyed."

"I've heard everything you said, Maxine, but I am still in the questioning stage. I need more physical proof that Atlantis really existed."

"That's what I've been trying to find for thirty years, Annie. I won't be satisfied until I locate a block of granite that says, 'Made in Atlantis!'"

"And what will you do with it?"

"Probably place it on the desks of my professors at U.C.L.A. and California State University, Northridge. Everyone doubted me. I faced so much ridicule in connection with Atlantis that I should have stopped searching for it years ago, but I just couldn't. I am obsessed with the subject."

"You know, Maxine, once in a while I have a vision of Atlantis. Your three spirals remind me of three Atlantean islands with a pyramid in the middle."

"Annie — would you believe I get over 1,000 letters yearly from people who also have visions of Atlantis? They draw the lost continent as well. There was even a two-year-old boy from Texas, named Jody Mosier, who could draw pictures of Atlantis as he remembered it."

"What about the Bible? What is the evidence there? You mentioned it earlier."

"Well, the Hebrews talk about the people of Ad, or the Adlans, who lived before the Flood. It's in the Talmud. The Book of Ezekiel speaks of the island in the sea. Possibly the Rock of Gibraltar is the rock around which the waters swirled in Psalms. Myths are very helpful too. The Navajos and Hopis tell of people coming out after a great flood. The Mexicans have a similar legend about Quetzalcoatl who came from Aztlan in the sea."

"There are other interesting facts about Atlantis. For example, we have common pyramids on both sides of the ocean, common burial practices, Egyptian characters in the Mayan alphabet and vice versa. Giant bones have been found on the Canary Islands of men almost twelve feet tall. The same bones were also found in Ireland. The large Canary Island bones of the Guanches may mean that these Indians were swift enough to climb to the tops of the mountains when the flood hit. The Canary Islands descend to the bottom of the ocean floor without a platform and may have been the mountains of Atlantis. Besides — remember what the Bible says, 'there were giants in those days.'"

"You mentioned Ireland. How does that country relate to Atlantis?"

"Ireland is a treasure trove of ancient artifacts. Professor Neville, of the University of Cork, placed Atlantis on his geologic map of Ireland. There are also language similarities between Spain and Ireland. The old name for Ireland was Hibernia. Spain was called Iberia. Coincidentally, the triple spiral boulder in front of the Caves of Newgrange in Ireland dates to 9600 B.C., the exact time of the holocaust. What is even more interesting, if you drop a string along a map from Ireland to Spain, you will see they lie on the same line of longitude. Both countries, I believe, are related to Atlantis."

"Well, if all this is true, where are the written records of Atlantis?" I asked.

"Annie — there are 5,000 undeciphered languages in the world. For all we know, one of them could be Atlantean. Edgar Cayce said the records were buried between the paw of the Sphinx and the Great Pyramid in Egypt. This is possible, since there is a 200-foot water mark at the top of Cheops Pyramid, meaning it might have been there before the Great Flood. Plato said he got his story of Atlantis from the Egyptian priests at the city of Sais near Alexandria. Cayce also said the other set of records is under the Pyramid of the Inscriptions in the temple at Palenque in Mexico. If that's true, then the survivors of Atlantis fled to both sides of the Atlantic when the holocaust came."

"In these major destructions, do people always survive?"

"Yes, Annie, they do. In any destruction, people may get a warning before the end comes. In ancient Pompeii, there were earthquakes and volcanic eruptions thirty years before the city was buried."

By this time, we were both tired, but nothing could stop Maxine once she started talking about Atlantis. She said, "Annie — there's another Atlantis possibility."

"What's that?" I yawned.

"Perhaps Atlantis was in Greece."

"Greece — in the Aegean Sea — why?"

"Well, in 1968, a Greek seismologist, Dr. Galanopolis, said he found Atlantis at Santorini, also called Thera, an island just north of Crete. His find dated to 1476 B.C. but Galanopolis claimed Plato had made a mathematical error by approximately 8000 years. I challenged him on this theory, but later Jacques Cousteau took an expedition to Greece and refuted the discovery as Atlantis. Unfortunately, a short time later, Dr. Galanopolis died, and later his aide, Dr. Marinatos, succumbed by falling into his own excavation. Perhaps Galanopolis was right about some of his theories, since Plato said the Atlanteans had a war with the Greeks. That could mean that Greece and Atlantis existed at the same time. After the flood, Greece may have emerged again.

"What are your plans now, Maxine?"

"Well, I hope to raise about five million dollars for a legitimate

Atlantis search. I certainly don't want to die impoverished, like the great Atlantean researcher, Dr. Egerton Sykes, editor of "Atlantis — the Antediluvian World." The book went into dozens of printings and Sykes was known the world over, yet he couldn't raise twenty cents for a cup of coffee. That's pathetic. He was one of the world's most renowned scholars on the subject.

"Why haven't you gone to National Geographic or the Smithsonian for funding?" I asked.

"I have, but Atlantis is still too 'way out' for them. That's why I founded the Ancient Mediterranean Research Association in 1972.

"Well, sign me up," I told her, "I want to learn all I can about the mysterious lost continent of Atlantis. Myth or reality — it's a fascinating subject."

CHAPTER VI.

Psychic Archaeology

We should not pretend to understand the
world only by the intellect; we apprehend it
just as much by feeling.

CARL GUSTAV JUNG

One of the most fascinating subjects in the world is archaeology. Who would not want to delve into the mysteries of the past? Yet, few people are trained to perform this painstaking task. Ordinary people rarely get a chance to explore the unknown and it is left to the scientists to uncover the wonders of our buried ancient treasures.

Psychic archaeology, on the other hand, can be carried out by someone with intuition and a keen sense of adventure. It is an exciting hobby for the layman, who seeks to discover something new about the ancient world, by "tuning in" to the force. I have friends in Arizona, the William Hinkleys, who have uncovered many ancient ruins in Cashan and other Indian sites, using a psychic approach. Bill Hinkley sometimes works with Tony Arlotta, an amazing psychic who locates artifacts by "seeing" through the ground. While Bill was digging in a Hohokan Indian site one day, exhausted and without any treasures, he spotted Tony, who stared at the twenty-foot trench Bill had dug.

He said, "Bill, the pot is right under your foot."

"It can't be," said Bill, "I've been digging in that spot for hours."

Tony furiously began to shovel away the sand. Sure enough, he uncovered a cremation burial in an olla (bowl) with another bowl inverted over the top. Bill stood there amazed. Tony had found artifacts again, using an intuitive approach. Now Bill is excavating in Eager, Arizona, where he has uncovered a unique Indian culture which dissected bodies of their dead before they buried them.

Psychic archaeology has a long history of success. In the late 1800s, a German businessman, Heinrich Schliemann, divorced his wife and left Germany for Greece, determined to find the mythical city of Troy, mentioned in Homer's classic epic, *The Iliad*. Schliemann was obsessed with Troy from boyhood on and carried copies of Homer's *Iliad* and *Odyssey* in his shirt pocket for reference. He met and married a Greek lady named Sophia whom he believed he had known in a past life. Together they went to a city called Hissarlik in Turkey. Schliemann hired a battery of workmen and, after examining the area carefully, walked up to a large mound and said, "Dig there." After several weeks of excavations, the workmen uncovered mythical Troy, buried under nine layers of other cities, believed to be later versions of the original. In the excavation were beautiful jewels and death masks of pure gold. Schliemann gathered all of these artifacts together and kept most of them for himself, giving only a few trinkets to the Turkish government. He then proceeded to decorate Sophia with the jewels since he believed she had worn them in a previous lifetime. Schliemann was a great believer in reincarnation and one of the most intuitive archaeologists who ever lived. Unfortunately, he was scoffed at by traditional scientists who insisted that what he found was not valid. This did not bother Schliemann since psychically he knew that this was the "real" Troy. Also in the excavation were remains of the original city, including evidence that the "Trojan Horse" had been real. Later Schliemann went on to excavate Tiryns and Mycenae in the same intuitive fashion, discovering the famous death mask of King Agamemnon of Mycenae, now in the museum of Athens. Schliemann was ahead of his time. He also had strong determination and a well-developed psychic ability. In later years, he was lauded by the same scientists who laughed at him at the time of the find. Thus his reputation and discovery were redeemed.

The city of Pompeii was also unearthed through a hunch. J. J. Winklemann, a German, knew psychically that Pompeii existed underneath thirty feet of silt somewhere near Naples, Italy. He and two friends started out to find Pompeii, based on Winklemann's feelings about the location, but he was murdered before he ever arrived at the site. Shortly afterward, his friends went on to uncover Pompeii, the discovery of which startled the 18th century world.

Then, in 1901, a prominent Englishman, Sir Arthur Evans, became enchanted with the Greek myth of "Theseus and the Minotaur." He believed he would discover the Palace of King Minos in Crete where the half-bull, half-man, Minotaur supposedly devoured eight Athenian girls and eight boys each year as tribute from King Aegeus. Using only the myth and his hunches as a guide, he discovered the palace and also the spiral labyrinth where the Minotaur had lived. His work was praised by scientists because Evans was "one of them." They never mentioned his use of intuition and mythology in making the find. Still, documents prove that his method was largely psychic throughout the difficult excavation.

One archaeologist who suffered mightily in the 19th century was Marcellino, who discovered the drawings in the Caves of Altamira in northern Spain. By intuition, Marcellino knew that the highly developed cave pictures were at least 20,000 years old. He brought other archaeologists into the cave but they insisted the pictures were more recent. In fact, they could not conceive of civilized man living as far back as 20,000 B.C. Marcellino would not change his hypothesis. For the rest of his life, he was shunned and ridiculed by his peers. He died in disgrace and disrepute, still insisting on the antiquity of the treasures. Several decades later, he was proven correct. Today we know that Cro-Magnon man painted those pictures from twelve to twenty thousand years ago.

Although the foregoing discoveries are quite spectacular, there have been other anthropologists and archaeologists who have used psychic approaches in their work. Dr. Jeffrey Goodman, in his book, *Psychic Archaeology,* demonstrated how the psychic approach worked for him. He gave examples from his own experience in the field. At a "dig" in Arizona with psychic Aron Abrahamson, Dr. Goodman watched while Aron located artifacts many feet under the ground where there was no visible sign of their location. He did this while University of Arizona officials and the press observed his psychic methods. Tony Arlotta also allows other people to observe his psychic work. He uncovered a spectacular Pima Indian burial mound while TV cameras rolled and reporters watched. Some psychics cannot operate under this kind of pressure. For example, the Israeli psychic Uri Geller could not bend metal while on the air. Yet many creative people use the psychic approach in their work in less spectacular ways.

A poll taken in 1975 asked anthropologists how often they used intuition in their research. Two hundred scientists were surveyed and it was reported that thirty-five percent of the respondents used an intuitive approach fifty percent of the time. Most scientists and inventors have psychic ability. Thomas Edison clairvoyantly "saw" the light bulb one day as he was shaving. After hundreds of rational experiments, the solution to Edison's problem came in a non-traditional way. This is not an unusual occurrence.

Certain sensitive individuals can learn to be psychic archaeologists. All it takes is an open mind, an interest in the ancient world, and the time to explore. It also requires money to travel. All of us have some inner thirst to be explorers. It is part of human nature, but we believe we cannot do these things because we haven't been trained in college. Psychic archaeology appeals to the adventurous spirit in us all.

It has been said that people's hunches, and memories of the past, may be more valuable than history itself. The Irish believe in myths and send "collectors" around the countryside each year to document the stories of their people. Myths and memories may be more reliable predictors of the past than history, since such knowledge comes from the "timeless" right brain. Historians embellish the facts of history with their own feelings. There is more bias in historical writing than in some mythologies and folk memories, which are man's direct understanding of the past. The Greek historian, Herodotus, fabricated his histories. Thucydides, who lived and wrote at the same time, was more objective, but still prejudiced some of his accounts.

Sometimes a dream or premonition can lead to a discovery. Henri Layard discovered the palace of Nimrud in Assyria, based on a clairvoyant dream. Layard tried to make the discovery for weeks through conventional means but couldn't find the right spot to dig. Then he had his dream. It was so accurate that workers found the palace instantly. The rest is history. Layard excavated one of the greatest finds the world has ever seen.

The purpose of psychic archaeology, I believe, is to locate "finds" that cannot be made through conventional means. A good psychic can "connect" with the energy of a "find," even if the site or artifact is completely covered over. When a psychic archaeologist makes a discovery, it is no coincidence. He is psychically drawn to it because he visualizes it in his "mind's eye" and connects with the energy of the artifact or site.

The following is a list of ideas that can help the amateur psychic archaeologist who wants to go out into the field. One must always clear the mind of distractions. The best method for that is through meditation. Of course, the researcher must have the financial means to travel and the motivation to succeed. Some guidelines to follow are:

1. Make sure the land you are working on is open to excavation. All countries, and all Indian lands in the United States, require permits to excavate.

2. Before working, meditate for at least fifteen minutes to clear the mind of excess energy. If possible, visualize the object you believe you might uncover.

3. If you sense an artifact is there, keep on digging until you find it. Don't give up. You might be closer than you think.

4. Evaluate your feelings and don't be in a hurry for the physical object to appear. There is a saying which says, "Awareness precedes physical manifestation."

5. If one site isn't productive, go on to another. Use intuition to guide your search.

Recently, in Sedona, Arizona, I went hiking on my land and something drew me to a certain spot on the ground. I looked down and there, by my right foot, was a perfect white Indian stone arrowhead. I was speechless. I showed it to a friend, who is with a museum, and he told me it was over 900 years old. The Sinaqua Indians formerly used my land as a camping site, and I will probably find pottery shards, and other artifacts as well, after a rain.

Psychic archaeology is one of the many ways you can apply mind power to accomplish a task. Above all, it should bring you into closer communication with the ancient ones, who are on the "other side."

CHAPTER VII.

The Psychic World

Ann Miller at Machu Picchu in Peru. Photo by Charlie See.

Co-stars Ann Miller and Mickey Rooney in "Sugar Babies."

Ann and Maxine Asher working on script at "Out of This World," 1990 TV show.

UFO sighted in Brazil, taken by three high school seniors on a biology field trip. Photo courtesy Brad Steiger.

Anna Mitchell-Hedges holding the famous Honduran Crystal Skull. Photo by Frank Dorland.

The Honduran Crystal Skull.

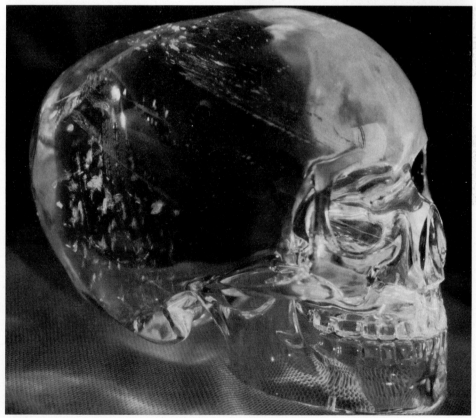

*At home in Sedona, with secretary Debbie Zehnder, pets
Cinderella and Jasmine, and Coffee Pot Rock in the background.*

Left to right: Naomi White Bear, Bill Garland, Ann, and White Bear at the Garland Jewelry Store in Oak Creek Canyon.

Ann at Giza, Egypt viewing Solar Boat.

Hatshepsut's Temple, Valley of the Kings, Luxor, Egypt.

Ann with a Moroccan gold merchant at Barbara Hutton's palace, holding the belt she felt was hers from another lifetime.

Dr. J. Manson Valentine taking a core sample of Atlantean blocks at Bimini.

Ann in the Valley of the Kings, Luxor, Egypt.

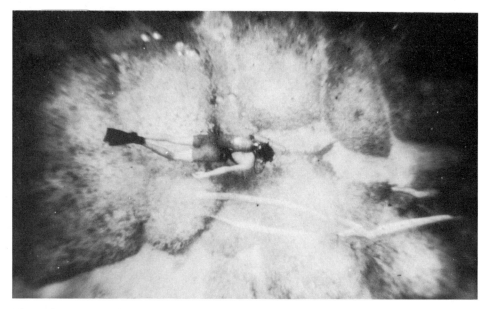

The Underwater Temple Blocks at Bimini, believed to be Atlantean.

Ann with Kamal El Malach, discoverer of the Solar Boat.

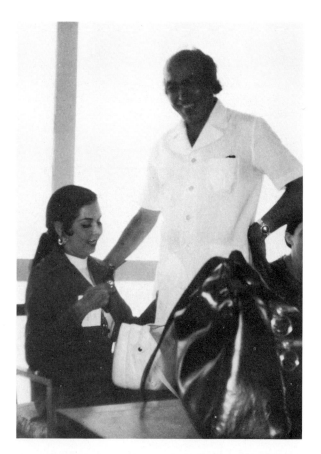

Ann in Nefertera's Tomb.

Dr. Maxine Asher and speleologist Vincent Meehan at the Spiralled Caves of Newgrange, Ireland.

Ann and Kathryn Grayson.

Left: Maurice Chevalier.
Center: Ann Miller.
Right: Ann's husband
Arthur Cameron.

Ann, Hermes Pan, and on the right Farah Diba, wife of the
Shah of Iran, at the palace in Teheran.

Ann and Princess Margaret of England in 1989.
Photo by Doug McKenzie.

*At the Palladium in London with Lord Delfont, the Queen
Mother, and Mickey Rooney, before the Royal Variety Show.
Photo by Doug McKenzie.*

With Patrick Swayze, receiving their Dance Awards of America Honor in the ABC-TV special, 1990. Photo by Scott Downie.

Ann with Shirley MacLaine, at Dance Awards of America. Photo by Scott Downie.

PHOTO BY RICHIE SPENCER

With long-time friend, impresario James A. Doolittle (left) and Dean Richard Toscan of U.S.C. drama department, presenting Ann, in March 1990, with a plaque honoring her career. Every year, a scholarship will be given in her name to the best drama student at U.S.C.

As the brain changes are continuous,...they are but one protracted consciousness, one unbroken stream.

WILLIAM JAMES

W ho would not want to predict the future? Everyone is curious about what lies ahead. I am no exception. Yet, I cannot always psychically help myself. So, when I have a problem, I sometimes go with friends to see an outstanding clairvoyant. Some of these psychics have been famous; others have not. Most of them were remarkably accurate but there are a few that stand out in my mind as being exceptionally good.

Dr. Mary Young was the first clairvoyant I ever encountered in Houston, Texas in 1936. In my opinion, she was one of the greatest psychic's of them all. She predicted I would go to Hollywood and begin a career that would last for years. She was absolutely correct. Even in the late thirties, after Mother and I left Texas, we were in touch with Dr. Young. We encouraged her to come to Los Angeles and she did. Many years later, we introduced her to a large number of well known stars and friends, and she made predictions for them. In 1948, a young girl who was in the movie "Easter Parade" with me, went to Dr. Young, who said she would meet and marry the movie star, Robert Stack. She also said it would be a long and happy marriage. The girl's name was Rosemarie Bowie. Dr. Young was right. Rosemarie met Bob and they are happily married to this day. Regarding my own romances, Dr. Young said I would not be happy in a marriage until later years. She also predicted I would not attain my greatest stardom until then. I was a very young girl when she said that and her statement depressed me. I didn't want to have to wait so many years for my dreams to come true. Little did I know that "Sugar Babies" would give me the stardom that Dr. Young had predicted. Regarding her observations about my love life, I have been patient, still hoping that "Prince Charming" will show up soon!

Maurice Woodruff, one of England's most famous psychics, came to my home in Beverly Hills around 1950, with friends. He said amazing things about my past and present life and predicted that my mother would have a lingering illness. She did. He also "saw" my success in the stage play, "Mame," on Broadway, which took place in 1969 and 1970. He has since passed on, but his psychic ability still lingers in my mind, as most of his prophecies were realized.

Peter Hurkos is a name that people know the world over. I met him at a Beverly Hills dinner party given by the noted actor Glenn Ford. Peter was one of the invited guests.

He came across the room and said, "Ann, you must be very careful about your chest. Air conditioning is bad for you especially when you ride in cars." How did Peter know that? It was absolutely true.

I said, "Thanks, Peter, I'll take your advice." He was correct. I had to be careful, not only in cars but in theaters and sound stages too. When air conditioning blew on me, I developed a flu-like condition in my chest and a cough. That would be great for singing, wouldn't it? Peter and I became friends that night. He was from Holland and spoke some English, but with a very heavy accent. He asked if I would drive him to the Ambassador Hotel in Los Angeles the following night after Glenn Ford's dinner party. He was scheduled to meet the press the evening we arrived, and I could see that he was nervous, perspiring heavily, and his hands shook. Since he could read people's minds, he hated to be in large crowds because he picked up so many different vibrations which drained him physically. Peter Hurkos was a true sensitive and crowds made him feel uncomfortable.

Just before his performance, Peter said, "Get me away from all these people so I can gather my energies together before the press reception. Can you find me a vacant room somewhere?"

"What kind of room?" I asked him.

"Anything at all — just a small room." I searched and searched but the only thing I could find was a big linen closet.

"Will this do?" I asked him, "can you fit in between all the linens?"

"Oh yes, fine," he answered. I was aghast. Poor Peter! When they called for him, I took him out of the closet and onto a small stage in a large convention room. The situation was so comical. There was the great Peter Hurkos, meditating in a linen closet at the Ambassador Hotel!

Peter not only had the gift of ESP and prophecy but of psychometry as well. Psychometry is the ability to touch an object and immediately know information about the owner and the object. Hurkos was a "smash" with the press and told them some fantastic things. First, he had everyone in the audience send up a personal object to the stage and he put them all together on a large tray which was placed on a table in front of him. Then he went through each object one by one, a piece at a time, and told the owners information about themselves. After he finished, each person was asked to come down to the stage to claim their watch, bracelet, rings, etc.

Everything was positive that night and Peter was accurate in his predictions. There was just one mishap. He picked up a key and said, "This belongs to a lady's apartment but the owner is a man." When he uttered that statement, the man came down to pick up his key and returned to his wife in the audience. Then Peter continued, "Strangely enough," he said, "that key does not belong to the man. It belongs to his mistress's apartment." The audience howled, but the wife slapped her husband and they left the auditorium screaming at each other on their way out of the hotel. According to published reports, Peter Hurkos became psychic when he fell four stories from a ladder while painting houses in Holland in 1941. He hit his head and was immediately clairvoyant from then on. His story is similar to the one told about Edgar Cayce, the "sleeping prophet," who also gained psychic abilities after a blow on the head.

Peter told me how the police called him in to solve many important crimes, including the "Boston Strangler" case and the "Manson Family" mass murders. In both of these cases, Peter said he gave officials the location of the guilty party or parties, which led police toward the ultimate solving of the crimes. Peter died in 1989, and the world has truly lost a great psychic.

Another clairvoyant whom I respect is Maria Moreno. I met her through Jess Stearn and learned that she channeled several entities. One was a Mexican hunchback, named "Pepe." "Pepe" spoke of money matters. The second entity was "Clarita," who gave advice on emotional and spiritual problems and romance. Finally, there was the elderly "Dr. Jallikete," who discussed health problems and their possible cures. Each of these beings had a different personality. Dr. Jallikete predicted I would have trouble with my eyes, which I did many years later. "Clarita" said I would marry a man who raised horses and was in politics. She said I would ride with this man and be thrown from the horse, which would result in a back injury. So far, none of these predictions have come to pass but then time is meaningless in the psychic world.

In 1980, when I was in "Sugar Babies" at the Mark Hellinger

Theater, my friend Shirley Eder, who is a noted newspaper columnist, brought Char, a young and attractive dark-haired woman backstage. She was a well known psychic and she asked to talk with me. She had just seen the show with Shirley and loved it. She proceeded to speak of my spirit guide John, who she felt was John the Baptist. Char said he was like a guardian angel who watched over me in this lifetime.

Char then spoke of my land in Arizona and said there would be a delay in the building of my dream home. She was right but I will build it. Since our first meeting, we have become good friends, and Char has since been in California. Each time we see each other, she makes predictions which seem to come true.

Once, at a dinner party at my home, she said, "I see an Indian chief behind you, Ann. He calls himself White Eagle." She also saw a white eagle hovering above the chief's head. Interestingly enough, I have an oil painting of an Indian chief named White Eagle hanging over my bed in Sedona with the eagle over his head. Char's ability to see all around me has to be more than coincidence.

In Sedona, I went to see psychic Ann Klein, a blonde housewife who channels an Arab man called HTP. Ann went into a trance, asking God to put a white light around us and help her guide me to the truth. The Arab entity spoke with a heavy accent. He was very enlightening and talked about past, present, and future lives. Ann Klein's psychic ability is very good. She tapes her sessions and gives the tape to the person experiencing the reading. Some of the things she predicted were helpful to me. For instance, she reaffirmed that I was an old soul and would not return again to this plane of existence. She said I had many lives in different areas and am guided by several Masters, especially a Hindu one. She also spoke of Sedona and said that the land I am building on is sacred Indian land.

She predicted that my troubles with my land would begin to be resolved later in 1988. I asked her who my spirit guide John was. She gave the same answer as Char, stating it was John the Baptist. I asked her if I would continue dancing and she said I would do so only when I wanted to, since now I had the freedom to choose. However, she predicted I would be a guiding light for other young dancers. She sees my future husband as a tall, white-haired man whom I will meet in London, and who will be financially secure. Ann Klein's predictions were fascinating. I will await the results of the reading in the months and years to come.

100

Another great psychic, Page Bryant, who wrote a book about the Sedona energy vortexes, gave me the best psychic reading I've had in years. In fact, all her predictions came true within a short period of time.

I was also impressed by Adele Tinning, an 82-year-old lady who lives in San Diego, mentioned in Shirley MacLaine's book and recommended to me by the famous mime, Robert Shields. When I heard about Adele, I immediately made the trip down to San Diego. She uses a table as a psychic tool and asks questions of it. The table raps one time for each letter of the alphabet and spells out the names of things! It also raps once for "yes" and twice for "no." When I sit with Adele, the energy is so powerful that the table moves with enormous force. She told me my master teacher was St. Thomas, and she also spoke of John. She said that St. Thomas was in the room with us and wanted to guide me.

Seeing Adele work the table was not new to me. As you recall, mother and I worked with a table in our home in Beverly Hills but, due to the appearance of negative forces, decided to abandon this.

Adele Tinning has an organization in San Diego called "God's Way of Life," and people come from all over the world to see this amazing lady and her table. She has been in touch with NASA, when one of the deceased astronauts, Ed White, sent a message to her via the table, using a coded alphabet. The message was about why the "Apollo" had crashed. Also, when the Voyager went to Mars, Adele told Bill Johanson at NASA that Ed White spoke to her from the other side and said,

"Don't land where you are planning to land. There is too much ice there." So they moved the landing spot over and were glad they did. NASA is very interested in Adele. She accepts no money. She does it all for the good of humanity.

There have been other psychics in my life. Tony Martin, the famous singer, came to see me and brought an East Indian prince called Prety Singh, along with the Maharajah of Cooch Bahar. The prince sat in my little den in my house and proceeded to read my hand. He said I would be married four times. My first husband would cause me to lose my child and my second would have three children. My third husband would have four children. All that information came true but when he said my fourth husband would have eight children, I almost went into cardiac arrest! Thank goodness that prediction hasn't happened yet.

Prince Prety Singh said my fourth husband would be my soulmate.

I hope he's right but this man had better come into my life quickly so at least I'll have time to enjoy the relationship! The prince reaffirmed that I am an old soul with many lifetimes, some in India. He said I would return there later in life, and I will.

One of my dearest friends, the noted writer, Jess Stearn, who has written many books about psychics, is well known in the metaphysical field. His book, *The Psychic Lives of Taylor Caldwell*, is outstanding, since he participated in Taylor's past life regressions during the writing of the book. After the regression, Ms. Caldwell questioned the information she gave under hypnosis, which included metaphysical statements and information about her life on the lost continent of Atlantis. Before the hypnosis, she said she didn't believe in reincarnation, but when the tape was played, she acknowledged uttering the words in a hypnotic state. It is possible that the historical knowledge used in her many books, including *Dear and Glorious Physician,* came from her intuitive memory of past lives, which made her writing so real and alive.

Early in my life I learned to be cautious when entering any phase of the psychic world. There are charlatans who take your money and may destroy your life in the process. When I do go to psychics, I write down their information in a little diary and put the book away in a drawer for future reference. Many show business people, like myself, have investigated psychic phenomena. For example, Linda Evans worked with Ramtha, and Sharon Gless has a great belief in the psychic Lazaris. Dennis Weaver is also an advocate of UFOs.

Real psychics don't operate like machines, "turning on the force" at will. It simply comes to them. Most sensitives are dedicated individuals who enjoy their work and want to help other people. The really good psychics I have known don't even charge for their skills. It is their gift from God and they share it freely with others. If any money is given, it is usually donated to research or a church.

In my opinion, if you need help or advice, it is better to go to a religious counselor, psychologist, or family member, rather than seeking the views of a psychic whose abilities are unknown to you. Better to be safe than sorry.

Speaking of psychics, the whole world recently connected with Nostradamus, a 16th-century soothsayer, who predicted that in 1988, a big earthquake would come to California in May and cause massive destruction. His predictions caused thousands of people to leave the state, including a whole colony of Orientals, whose own psychic predictions matched those of Nostradamus. The great seer claimed a certain planetary alignment would cause a massive earthquake. The quake did not come in May of 1989. But a large quake occurred in the San Francisco area in October of 1989. Nostradamus foresaw the rise of Hitler, and the fall of the Shah of Iran, as well as the Kennedy assassination. These predictions were all made through the use of his clairvoyant powers. Nostradamus has been dead 422 years. Perhaps his intuition about the massive quake in California will be right. Only time will tell.

Remember, when you decide to go to a psychic, do so with pen and paper in hand and a healthy bit of skepticism in your consciousness. Carefully choose your psychic or medium and remember the information you receive may or may not be true. Just put it in your favorite "hiding place" for future reference, and see if the events come to pass.

CHAPTER VIII.

Crystals, Gemstones, and the Crystal Skull

The crystal shines like the eternal star,
lighting up the sky and all eternity.

MARTIN MILLAR

Throughout the ages, women have coveted beautiful gemstones, precious minerals, and sparkling bits of crystal. They have treasured this natural wealth from beneath the earth and, in their greed, sometimes killed to possess gold and jewels. Cleopatra had her emerald mines. The land of "Punt" was known for its silver and a rare greenish gold. King Solomon's mines are still a mystery to historians of the ancient world, and Sheba, Queen of Saba, adored gems and precious metals. Even King Nebuchadnezzar of Babylon decorated his wives with precious jewels. Is it any wonder then, that in this day and age, women continue to value colorful gemstones and brilliant crystals just as their sisters did in earlier times?

I am a rock hound. I collect ancient pieces of earth with snails and fish inside, which are millions of years old. I buy amethyst geodes to place in my home, since I believe they are filled with energy and beauty. Being a woman, I am interested in beautiful polished gemstones too. Wherever I travel, I try to bring back loose stones and jewelry which I buy for their appearance and color. I have consulted the experts about the meaning of crystals. I own one which I keep on my body. I am told it keeps my spiritual energy intact. It was a gift from a friend. As I was curious about the function of crystals, I consulted with internationally known crystal expert, Frank Dorland.

I asked him, "Frank, why is the crystal, an ancient gemstone, so important to 'New Age' people?"

"Because the electronic quartz crystal develops the higher vibrations of the mind, and the psychic senses."

"I wear a crystal, but I'm not sure what to do with it. How does it work?"

"The electronic quartz crystal works with the mind, Ann. This crystal transmits energy when it receives a signal from our own consciousness. Crystals are not only used by psychics. They are important in the computer industry, in watch manufacturing, and in radio and television sets. Our whole modern civilization is based on communication, which depends on the use of the crystal. The electronic quartz crystal transmits and receives energy which works with the human mind, the subconscious, and the body cells. Some hospitals use modern machinery which employs the crystal. This is called resonance imaging."

"Then how can I use a crystal?" I asked him.

"Just program it — tell it what you want it to do."

"You mean talk to the crystal — is that what I am supposed to do?" At this point, the whole idea sounded rather weird.

"Yes, that's right. Just hold one in your right hand and rest it in your left hand. Then tell it what you want it to do."

This was "way out," I thought, but after all, Frank was the expert. After speaking to him, I started talking silently to my crystal, asking it to give me energy. Later, I learned from reading that crystals are living, growing objects and that they can broadcast waves received by the body and mind. That is why fortune tellers used crystals for ages. Sometimes ancient people also placed them in temples, pyramids, and sacred sites. Crystals are part of the "New Age" movement.

I not only wear a crystal on my body, but keep many in my home as objects of beauty. I also read that psychic healers use crystals to cure people. They line them up along the body's energy centers (chakras), and then the healer uses power of mind to send energy through the crystal to the person's body. This magnifies the energy and increases its healing capability. I cannot personally attest to this process, because I have never been to a healer. When I am sick, I usually go to my family doctor! However, if you believe in the power of crystals, your own mind energy will work with the crystal to help heal your body. I am more interested in crystals and gemstones for their beauty and mystical qualities, than I am in their purported healing nature. Sometimes I choose jewelry that reminds me of a past lifetime. When I was in Morocco, I searched for a small gold wedding belt, which brides brought to their husbands in ancient times, as part of their dowry in marriage. I trekked through twenty to thirty stores in the Casbah on the "Street of Gold," since my friend, Marcia Israel of Los Angeles, told me where to buy one. She is very close to the royal family of Morocco and knew that I would love this beautiful work of ancient art, still made today by the gold craftsmen of Morocco.

My friend and accountant Joan Gibson, Debbie, and I were staying at Barbara Hutton's palace, "Sidi Hosni." One afternoon we went into the Casbah with the houseboy, Hassiz. I searched and searched for the gold belt. When I finally saw the one I wanted, I had strange feelings about it. I felt I had worn one before, just like it, in a previous lifetime. Yet the owner of the shop would not bargain with me, which is the custom of Moroccan shop owners. I was puzzled. The belt was a high-priced piece of jewelry and the owner wouldn't come down on the price. As I looked into his eyes, trying to get him to lower the fee, I became mystified with what I saw. His eyes were like black limpid pools, and his beard and dark robes mesmerized me. I felt like I was reliving a scene from the days of Christ, that I had done all this before. I could sense that he was a very honest man. I went back to the store three times and tried to bargain. I did this because, in Arab countries, the first price asked is never the selling price. I knew most shopkeepers are not insulted when customers try to bring the price down. This man, however, was adamant. I finally agreed to pay the full amount he was asking and he promised to bring the belt to the palace for payment. My friend Joan said, "Ann, you are crazy. No one spends this kind of money just for a silly belt. I don't care how much gold is in it. You don't need it."

"Joan," I told her emphatically, "I do need it. It belongs to me. I feel I wore this belt in a past life." Joan glanced at Debbie and both of them stared back at me in amazement. I looked at the belt again. It had small diamonds and emeralds on the buckle. From the first moment I saw it, I felt it was mine from another lifetime in the Middle East. I offered the shopkeeper traveler's checks in payment. He said, "I don't take traveler's checks."

"I can't believe that," I told him. "They are just like cash and I don't have that much money with me."

"Sorry, I don't take them." I looked at my watch.

"O.K." I grumbled, "We'll go to the bank and get you your cash." I was determined to buy the belt. I told him we would all meet back at the palace.

Joan and I went to the bank and took a satchel with us for this huge stack of Moroccan money. We brought it back to the palace. Then she and the shop owner counted every bill together, one by one. By this time, it was 7:30 at night. The shop owner was perspiring profusely. This was a lot of money for him to be carrying home so late at night. Joan was grimacing with fatigue. Finally, the shopkeeper said, "You could have given me a personal check." At that comment, Joan almost picked up the nearest vase and hit me over the head with it. I never thought to ask him about a "personal check." That was too easy. The whole situation was very comical to me, but not to Joan. After the transaction, we all had mint tea and took pictures. Because of his religion, the shopkeeper would never look directly into the camera for fear of losing his soul. Most of all, I had my belt, and that was one of the best things that happened to me on my whole trip to Morocco. I know I'll always remember the experience of purchasing this ancient and beautiful work of art.

One of the most unusual crystal artifacts in the world is called the "Crystal Skull." It was discovered in 1927 by Mitchell-Hedges in Honduras and was first recorded by Richard Garvin in his book, *The Crystal Skull.* The skull was used for ancient religious rites and had a lower jaw that was hinged and worked by priests who stood behind it unseen. Thus, it literally "talked" to the people.

I went to a lecture in Sedona, Arizona and heard Ann Mitchell-Hedges, the daughter of the discoverer, tell about the skull, which I was able to view. It is fashioned from a solid piece of crystal, perfect in every detail. Even Frank Dorland couldn't find any tool marks in his microscopic examination of it. Frank thinks the skull was hand rubbed into its present form, but such a job could have taken more than 200 years. Ms. Mitchell-Hedges keeps the artifact in Canada, except when she is on the road lecturing. She was present at the discovery and is very serious about its value. Her father believed it was an artifact from Atlantis and was actually looking for Atlantis when he found it. Ms. Mitchell-Hedges is not "caught up" in the current crystal frenzy that is sweeping our country. She sees the skull only as an artifact. Here is what she wrote to Dr. Asher on April 6, 1988:

"Dear Dr. Asher:
I was at the Cayce Foundation with the Crystal Skull in 1984 and found it a most peaceful place to visit. My father is mentioned in Edgar Cayce's book on Atlantis, which he believed was in Central America...that is how he found the citadel in the heart of the jungle which is named Lubaantun (Place of the Fallen Stones). It took seven years to clear because we had to burn as we went. I was out climbing the stones one day when I saw something shining. I told my father (what I had seen) but he said it was probably a piece of glass. Later, he decided it could be something else and got the men to move the stones which took two men to lift. It was then we found

the top (of the skull) and I was sent down to collect it. Some three months later, we discovered the jaw. Having seen the faces of the Mayans, father said,

"This is something we cannot take away," and gave it back to the Mayans, who built an altar for it. When we finished our expedition some two years later, the Mayans returned it to my father because he had been so kind to them and they said it would be quite safe with him. That is why it is in my possession today. Had we taken it away when I brought it out of the ruins it would have been given to either the Museum of the American Indian or the British Museum, and it would have been kept under shatter proof glass and not given pleasure to so many people...I take it to conferences with the expedition slides and now I have a video of the Mayans helping on the expedition. They remember us, and they also say the Crystal Skull belongs to the whole world and that everyone should be crystal minded. This is in their own language but is translated by a younger man. I have two friends who sat talking with them all on the ruins of Lubaantum. They were also allowed to video some of the native dances and a tree cutting ceremony. They do not want the Crystal Skull returned because eventually they would lose it and they would prefer it did the work it is doing now. We get many healings and many people have said it has completely changed their lives."

Ms. Mitchell-Hedges also said that people came to her in Canada in 1985 and observed the energy of the skull, which they said extended out 300 yards toward the street. Ms. Mitchell-Hedges worked very closely with Frank Dorland and his wife Mabel. In fact, she loaned the Crystal Skull to the Dorlands for observation. They had it for six years. In *The Crystal Skull*, Frank Dorland was quoted as saying, "The first night they kept the skull overnight in their home, they were awakened by unusual noises in their house, including a jungle cat, silver bells tinkling softly, and chimes. The next morning, possessions were scattered all over their living room, yet all the windows and doors were locked. At other times, they heard what sounded like music or human voices, singing strange chants. The skull also gave off what Frank called "an illusive perfume or odor". They would see many pictures and images appearing within the skull. These images included other crystal skulls, high mountains, temples, and faces, which Frank was even able to photograph. On several occasions, Frank remembered seeing a dark spot, which would spontaneously appear within the Crystal Skull and grow in size until it would fill at least half of it. During this process, the skull's temples would repeatedly disappear and reappear. His most profound experience occurred one evening when he was looking at the skull and he noticed a glow or aura appearing around it. At this time, the crystal skull was in ordinary light, when suddenly this aura appeared and grew until it was a full eighteen inches surrounding the skull. This phenomenon lasted six minutes. He didn't believe what he was seeing so he picked up a magazine and read a few words in order to refocus his eyes. When he looked back at the skull, the aura was still there and it intensified, This experience taught him a great deal about the auras encircling all living things. Based on his research, he feels that the skull was put to a religious use, with by the Atlanteans ancient Egyptians, Babylonians, or even the Tibetans."

The history of crystal and jewelry has always fascinated me. I collect replicas of ancient designs, especially Greek, American Indian, and Egyptian. I love both silver and gold. I am especially interested in the metal the ancient Egyptians used, called "electrum," which was gold and silver mixed. I don't believe this metal exists today. Hatshepsut said it shone like the sun. The queen used electrum on her obelisks and her monuments.

The American Indian uses silver and gold and turquoise, which is a derivative of copper. Turquoise is worn on their chests for decoration and they believe it helps cure arthritic pains. I adore turquoise and wear lots of it. Gazing at the stone is like looking into the magnificent blue of a sky. Aquamarine is like a deep blue lake, and tourmalines make me feel happy and peaceful. They come in many lovely colors. Rubies, on the other hand, because of their blood-red hue, remind me of roses and make me feel romantic and sensuous. Emeralds are exotic and mysterious. Yes — I am a true rock hound!

I would never advise anyone to buy jewelry with a curse on it, like a scarab or the Hope Diamond. Most people can't afford to anyway, so it makes a good excuse! Even crystals, I learned, can have unpleasant vibrations. I saw a friend wearing a crystal pendant. Several weeks later she stopped wearing it. I asked, "Where is the crystal necklace your friend gave you in San Diego? I never see you wearing it anymore."

She said, "It brought me bad luck."

"But why didn't you clear it? I've heard you can do that with crystals," I asked her.

"I tried, Ann — I really did. I talked to it but the energy of the previous owner was just too powerful and negative for me."

"Where is it now?" I asked.

"I threw it down the incinerator." I nearly choked.

"Why did you do that?"

"I didn't want it anywhere near me," she said. I pondered why anyone would throw a beautiful crystal necklace down an incinerator. Later, I found out that if a piece of jewelry or a crystal is causing some disturbance, or a bad memory, in your life, you must get rid of it. Of course, that could be costly, depending on the value of the object, but it's never a good idea to possess something that has an unpleasant vibration. For example, an old wedding band, or a wedding dress, should be sold or given away rather than kept after a separation or divorce.

Crystals have been around for a long time. The ancients used crystals for the same reasons we do because they understood that the earth, like the human body, has energy centers, called ley lines. At Stonehenge in England, and at the Pyramid of Cheops in Egypt, crystals have been found. It is believed they may have been used for power, for divination (fortune telling) or for communication, similar to the function of the Crystal Skull. Psychics say there is a giant crystal under the town of Sedona, Arizona. Perhaps that is one of the reasons people feel so energized there.

Sometimes the energy of a stone is irresistible. When I attended the World's Fair in Vancouver, there was a citrine stone from Sri Lanka on exhibit. It was 365 carats, and was only on display. I felt again that this stone, or a similar one, had belonged to me in a past life. Once more, over the repeated objections of my accountant Joan, who was with me, I bought the stone. Now I wear it only with caftans on very special occasions. It has amazing vitality. Joan thinks I am very peculiar at times. Perhaps I am. However, I treasure and keep valuable things all my life.

Speaking of crystals and gemstones, by this time you may be wondering what crystal is made of and where it comes from. Most people know about crystal goblets at the table but are not familiar with crystal as a gemstone. Actually, the chemical name for quartz crystal is silicone dioxide and its common form is called silica. Some silica gemstones are beryl, zircon, carnelian, agate, sardonyx, jasper, amethyst, garnet, lapis lazuli, opal, and topaz. One of the most beautiful of all these stones is pure rock crystal. It is grown in the depths of the earth and takes thousands of years to form. These crystals change colors when exposed to light because they are many-faceted. They look like huge diamonds, and people in the ancient world valued the two stones equally.

Although modern business and industry have their own uses for crystals, such as ensuring accuracy in timepieces, currently the psychic world has taken up the ancient practices. Crystals have always been good-luck pieces throughout history they continue to be so today. Purchase one yourself and see if it works for you.

CHAPTER IX.

Sedona — The Red Rock Shangri-La

The native American shared this elementary ethic...the land was alive to his loving touch, and he, its son, was brother to all creatures...

STEWART LEE UDALL

My romance with Sedona started in 1978. Located in Arizona's red rock country, this Shangri-La village of 12,000 people, 4,500 feet high, is surrounded by bright red mountains, breathtaking in their beauty. Sparkling green trees, fleecy white clouds, and starry nights complete the majestic panorama. To me, Sedona is Shamballa. It's a glorious place. Shamballa is a sanskrit word meaning a meeting place of all beings, animals, and humans in peace. A *Los Angeles Times* travel writer, who recently visited Sedona, described it like this: "The mesas and monoliths of this vast sculpture garden are mostly sandstone. Erosion has shaped them into bells and cathedrals, teapots and layer cakes. Some are a thousand feet tall. At sunset they blaze like a hungry hearth; at dawn they glow like coals. Burnt red, cool pine green, and skies of Navajo turquoise...that's the palette of Sedona."

My first glimpse of Sedona came during my appearance in a play in Scottsdale. On my day off, I drove to the area with Debbie and my dogs, Cinderella and Jasmine. It was Sunday and we arranged to stay at the Poco Diablo Resort, where I rented a villa. As soon as we arrived, I walked out onto the golf course and saw the strange brilliant red mountains. I said to Debbie, "I'm going to have a home here someday. I feel as if I've come home, the same way I felt in Luxor, Egypt."

She looked at me with a patronizing smile but went along with my prediction. Little by little, I began to spend more leisure time in Sedona. During the run of "Sugar Babies," I would fly into Los Angeles and go on to Sedona to relax and charge up my batteries. It became an "inner sanctum" to me. Through a friend, realtor Bea Dunlap, I met the famous white Indian trader, Don Hoel, and his lovely wife Nita. The couple collect and sell beautiful Indian jewelry, rugs, and artifacts. They took Debbie and me to dinner and we spoke of the many big Indian tribes in the surrounding area: the Apache, the Hopi, and the Navajo. In ancient times, the Anasazi (meaning the old ones), the Hohokam, and the Sinagua tribes also lived here. Don Hoel told me that when members of a tribe became ill, they were brought to Sedona to be healed. They also came here for sacred ceremonies and pow-wows. Perhaps the ancients felt the same sense of wonderment and awe that I felt in seeing this magical place for the first time.

The Hoels have a lovely home, high up in Oak Creek Canyon, which, after leaving Sedona, is only a few miles beneath Flagstaff. This drive is one of the most beautiful in the world, with its rust red mountains, green trees, and waterfalls. Oak Creek snakes around six or seven times as you cross it up the switchbacks. When you arrive in the Flagstaff area, you see the San Francisco Mountains, which are even more beautiful in the wintertime with their snow-capped peaks.

Ironically, in all this splendor, the two greatest white Indian traders of all, Don Hoel and Clay Locket, were killed on the same road in car accidents within a short time of each other. Don, of course, was world famous for his collections of kachinas and outstanding Indian jewelry and rugs. In his younger years, Don introduced electricity into the Oak Creek Canyon area and at the instant of his death, all the lights went out in the canyon and stayed out for three hours! Clay Locket owned a well-known Indian collection and a shop in the Northern Arizona Museum. He also owned the land the museum was built on. Artifacts of great value were sold in his store, and people from all over the world came to see it and buy the treasures from him.

The Hopi Tribe around Flagstaff, Arizona feel that the San Francisco peaks are the sacred home of their "kachinas" or spirits. This entire area is Indian country and one can feel it. Rumor has it that a resort, recently built in Sedona on sacred Indian ground, enraged the Indian people so much they put an ancient curse on it. Strangely enough, the resort is not a big success, although the owners have worked hard to make it so, and it has since been sold three different times.

In Sedona, I have a strong sense of "deja vu," of having lived there before. Many psychics and sensitives live in the area because apparently there are powerful force fields of energy coming from the iron ore content in the rust red mountains. The vortexes (magnetic power centers) include Coffee Pot Rock, Bell Rock, Airport Mesa, and Boynton Canyon. Perhaps it is these centers that give me the sensations I feel because I am a sensitive. My present home is located right by Coffee Pot Rock. The county built barriers to try to protect these sites, but people came to them anyway to meditate and tune into the strong energy vibrations. During the recent "Harmonic Convergence" in 1987, people flocked to Sedona by the thousands and gravitated to the magnetic vortexes. These energy centers also exist in other parts of the United States and the world. They include Chaco Canyon, New Mexico; Spain; Kauai; Tangier; the Great Pyramid on the Giza Plateau in Egypt; and Stonehenge in Great Britain. The area around Sedona was under water millions of years ago. On top of the mountains, scientists (as well as some of my friends) have found fossils of animals, sea shells, and fish.

In Sedona, I am 'up and at 'em' by 6:00 in the morning. Even if I am physically tired, I still have an abundance of energy. In Los Angeles, I sleep until 9:00 a.m. The Sedona area affects my vitality and state of mind in a positive way.

Many great western artists live in this beautiful place. The Cowboy Artists of America is an organization formed in Sedona. It includes Sedona artists Jim Reynolds, Joe Beeler, Frank McCarthy, and Ray Swanson. Obviously, the beauty and timelessness of Sedona attracts them like a magnet. A large number of talented musicians also live in Sedona — it is a mecca for creative and sensitive people.

Recordings have been made of native Americans playing the flute, an ancient instrument. The melodies are handed down from their ancestors. I like nothing better than sitting in my living room, around five in the afternoon, feasting my eyes on the glorious red mountains, while the sun is setting, listening to a flute recording of ancient Indian melodies. My mind seems to travel backward into time, and I sense a deep peace and quiet that I have not found anywhere else on earth.

My interest in the native American tribespeople has allowed me to meet a number of other great white Indian traders like Bill and Dan Garland and Gordon Wheeler, who are authorities on Indian jewelry, baskets, pottery, and rugs. I have collected many of these beautiful Indian works of art from them to put into my home and have watched the Indian people as they worked on them. The Navajo specialize in the weaving of rugs. It is almost a lost art. I observed them as they put a story into each design, leaving a break in the weave of the rug for their spiritual soul to escape. The Navajo, like the Hopi, are very religious people. Their sand paintings all have to do with their spirit world and are very beautiful. In Navajo religious ceremonies, sand paintings that are created are later destroyed. I was told that when I went to buy a sand painting on a rug, or as a picture, it would not be a religious one with mystical significance. It would simply be a lovely painting since the originals are destroyed by the tribe.

The house I live in is an authentic adobe, seventeen years old and of Mexican design. The former owner had a Hopi chief and a Hopi medicine man bless it while he was building it. He then had them put special sacred fetishes into the house, which were buried in the cornerstones. The house sits in the middle of 13 3/4 acres with a fantastic view. Before I purchased it, I was taken several times by the real estate people to look it over. When I walked in the last time, I felt a deep sadness and a strong presence of the Indian people. The agent told me the man who built it had a young son who died and the father was grief-stricken. He built a small kiva (Indian word for prayer house) away from the main house where he would go to be alone. He meditated and prayed for his son with the help of his close friends, the Hopi medicine man and the Hopi chief. When I first saw the little house, it was filled with rubble left by the previous owner. They had abandoned their lapidary equipment, fishing boots, tackle, and a number of other personal items. I had the kiva cleaned and found that it had a small fireplace and a built-in bookcase, as well as wonderful old floors and big vigas (logs) on the ceiling. I told my real estate people that I was going to call this my "meditation room." They looked at each other and said, "That's strange, the man who built this kiva house years ago also called it his 'meditation room.'" My psychic antenna was working overtime again.

Many marriages break up in Sedona because of the intense energy fields. If a person has a fault, it seems to be magnified. Possibly the Indians understood this special force and came here for healing and energy and purification. One thing is certain. You will learn the truth about yourself if you come to stay in this vital land.

The Indian people particularly interest me because of their deep spirituality and healing abilities. For thousands of years, Indians have purified the body through the use of "sweat lodges" where they go to perspire and rid themselves of toxins. They also use roots and herbs, and the venom of snakes, for healing. Most important, the Medicine Man conducts mysterious ceremonies in which ancient incantations are used to speed the healing process.

Another part of native American mysticism is the symbol of the eagle. The eagle represents strength and imparts a "God-like" quality to the tribe. Such mysticism was stated in a religious booklet, *the Daily Word*, which my Indian ancestors would enjoy:

"We can, by entering a quiet place and 'listening' learn heaven's secrets while our lives on earth are fulfilling a phase of eternity."

Besides strength, the eagle has other symbology for the Indian people. The chiefs and braves wear eagle feathers since the eagle soars close to the heavenly spirits. The eagle is also free and independent, and imparts these qualities to the Indian people, who wear the beak and feathers for adornment during their religious ceremonies. The eagle is used in different functions, including personal decoration and re-creations of the bird's soaring spirit in dance.

Hopi beliefs are part of the magic of Arizona. Their mystical religion is similar to the Egyptians of ancient times. I had the pleasure of meeting White Bear Fredericks, elder of the Hopi tribe, whose father and grandfather were both Hopi chiefs. White Bear is often interviewed about his knowledge of the Hopi people, and the interviews appear in books on native American history. He has a lovely wife, Naomi, who assists him in his work. His clan is the Bear Clan. He makes his living by painting pictures of Hopi ceremonies as well as carving kachina dolls, 98 of which are in the Heard Museum in Phoenix. He also collaborated with Frank Waters on the *Book of the Hopi*.

White Bear believes that the Hopis are the oldest people in the universe. Originally, he states, his ancestors came from outer space. The Indians saw these men and carved their likeness into kachinas. The Hopis believe we are now living in the fourth world. Their history, they say, precedes the Chinese and even the Egyptians.

I arranged a lunch with White Bear in April of 1988 while I was in Sedona. He had some fascinating stories to tell about his people. He also discussed spiritual subjects and said, "There is a keyhole door that exists in various places in South America, and at the Pyramid of the Moon in Mexico City. It is the entrance to the spiritual world, which means universal consciousness. There was a keyhole door in an Egyptian pyramid and a twelve-year-old Pharaoh, now buried there, was the only one who knew where it was." White Bear also spoke about his friend, Erich Van Daniken, famous for writing *Chariots of the Gods* and other books on ancient archaeology. The two men believe the Hopis came from outer space. White Bear said he was also an archaeologist. He found a one-mile figure of a man made of stone in the Mojave Desert, which was photographed many times and is featured in books. When White Bear discovered this huge artifact, he said he was guided by a psychic voice. He also found a similar stone with petroglyphs which has a replica of the one-mile figure of the man carved on it. According to White Bear, the rock proclaims the Hopi's inheritance as the first people on earth.

One Hopi problem, as with all tribes, is that some younger members of the clans are pulling away from the "old ways" with the pressures of modern society. White Bear and Naomi try to keep the old customs alive. She is of English descent. She helps White Bear in the writing of his books. She also designs hats, dresses, and jackets, which are hand embroidered by her with White Bear's Hopi designs. My relationship with both White Bear and his wife has been a rewarding one.

I went to the Hopi reservation to see the sacred, long-haired Kachina Dance. To keep the ancient ceremonies, dances, and customs alive, the Indians perform them on a regular basis, but the public is rarely invited. No photographs or tape recordings are allowed. On the day that I observed the dance, the tribe was dressed as masked warriors, chanting and dancing to the beat of drums. It was an awesome sight, as if time had stood still. I was with a group of friends. We were on the First Mesa and there we met the world-famous potter, Rodina Huma, to whom I was introduced in Santa Fe at the Indian Art Show in August, where I bought a piece of her beautiful pottery.

No matter how important the Hopis become in the outside world they always return home to their reservation. They are very close and secretive as a tribe regarding their religion, beliefs, and ceremonies. Outsiders may no longer see the Snake Dance. The public seems to forget that to the Hopi, and all tribes, these dances are their religion. Loud talking, laughing, and grabbing at costumes is forbidden. We would not permit this in our own churches, so we should also respect the Hopi's views and all the wishes of the Indian tribes.

Unfortunately, many disrespectful incidents have occurred with the public, causing the Hopis to shut the door on some outside viewing of their religious ceremonies. I love Indian dances. In New Mexico, I was lucky enough to see the Buffalo Dance at the Cochiti Pueblo and to meet noted Indian potters, Helen Cadero and Mary Trujillo. In Santa Fe, I stayed at the well-known Rancho Encantado. Betty Egan is the owner. Mary Trujillo and her husband invited Debbie, Betty, and me to lunch at her house at the Cochiti Pueblo and we accepted. Betty Egan is very interested in Indian culture. When we went into Mary's house, we saw a decorative piece of pottery of a little Indian boy playing a drum. I went over to it and said, "I love this piece, Mary. How much is it?"

She said, "Sixteen fifty."

I said, "That's fine. I'll take three of them; one for Deb, one for Betty, and one for me." Betty pulled me aside and said,

"Annie, she means one thousand, six hundred and fifty dollars." I gasped.

I said, "On second thought, I think I'll take only one." Everyone laughed.

The pueblo tribes have many famous potters. One is Lucy Lewis, now in her eighties, of the Acuma tribe, and Margaret Tafoya of the Santa Clara tribe. Maria Martinez and her husband Julio, now deceased, made the famous black pottery with intricate designs of the San Ildefonso tribe.

Along with the making of pottery, Indian tribes like the Hopi and Zuni, excelled in the carving of excellent kachinas made out of a single piece of cottonwood. Each one made by the Hopis represents a spirit God. Some are ogres, some are white or black buffalo, others are deer dancers, sun kachinas, chasing star kachinas, sheep kachinas, etc.

On a recent trip to Gallup, New Mexico, a Catholic priest took Debbie and myself to the Zuni Reservation, into their Catholic church. I was amazed at the altar with its large holy crucifix in the middle with two huge black buffalo heads on each side. All around the top of the church, kachina spirits were painted and the Indians worshiped them along with the laws of Catholicism. It was obvious that the old ways prevailed side by side with Christianity.

I have spent many hours watching the Indians make their jewelry. Besides kachinas, the Hopis, the Navajos, and Zunis are famous for their jeweled creations. The Zunis do beautiful inlay work of turquoise, mother of pearl, coral, lapis, and silver. The Navajos work mostly with turquoise, silver, lapis, and some coral. They do heavy silver settings and modern gold settings with diamonds. This tribe apparently were nomads and most likely the descendants of the Mongolians. The Hopis believe in the spiritual world and are in daily contact with it. Like the Egyptians, the Hopis pray to the rising and setting sun. Everything in their world tells a story related to nature and to the spiritual forces. Their pottery and silver jewelry express this.

My interest in the native American people is a deep and sincere one, because of my Cherokee heritage. I believe all Indian people have

123

been treated unfairly and that something should be done to correct what happened in the past and give them the honor they deserve.

The people of Sedona are wonderful and I have made many friends there. Some of them believe in the idea of life after death. In fact, most people in Sedona have a psychic and spiritual orientation, and quite a few of them support the idea of reincarnation. My friends Bea and Everett Dunlap do. Everett, a former white Indian trader and collector, talks to his spirit guide "Charlie." His wife Bea, now deceased, bought a new Cadillac but Everett wouldn't get into it. Charlie told him not to do so. Subsequently, the wife had a terrible accident, and "totaled" the car. She came out with only minor injuries. Then she bought a second car and Charlie told him it was all right for Everett to ride in that one and he does just that. In another case, Charlie advised Everett about a man who owed him a lot of money but didn't have it. Charlie told him not to worry because the money would be given to him on a certain date. On that date, the man called from England and said, "Your check is in the mail."

Another friend, Gladys Hogue, had an incredible experience after her mother and father died. She woke up and they were in the same room with her. They smiled and then slowly disappeared. She has never forgotten that scene.

There are a lot of people who do not verbalize mystical experiences because of their fears, or the fact that people will think they are having a nervous breakdown. I am not concerned about stating what I have experienced, because I know these things really happened. You see, I am somewhat superstitious and had an experience in Sedona which reinforced my beliefs. When I first bought my present home, Debbie, the dogs, and I were ready to go out the kitchen door when suddenly a big snake came slithering across, right in front of the door. Debbie jumped back, slammed the door and yelled, "Watch out." The dogs were with us and we could see, with terror, a large snake, ambling right past us. I said to Debbie, "This snake is warning me that a lot of enemies and problems are coming our way concerning this land but something will happen to reverse all this."

She said, "Ann, you really are bonkers!" Later, it was demonstrated that my perception of this warning was right. Since that time, I have resolved my problems with the land, but the symbol of the snake clearly spelled out his warning to me loud and clear. Perhaps my Indian heritage sensed this.

People have asked what I do when I am in Sedona besides pursuing my abiding interest in the Indian people and their history. I like to read, listen to music, walk into the mountains with the dogs, watch the sunsets, and observe the wildlife, especially the eagles and the ravens. Since the eagle represents a soul in flight, transcending the world on the power of its wings, watching the eagles flying, brings me closer to God.

I am never bored in Sedona. I have so many friends, and because my spiritual nature is encouraged in this wonderful village, I decided to build a Santa Fe style vacation home there. I feel lucky to have found my own "inner sanctum." Everyone has their special place and Sedona is mine.

CHAPTER X.

Developing Right-Brain Energy

Scorn not your powers as if proportionate to the smallness of the mind: its power has no bounds.

MARCUS MANILIUS

 One Friday afternoon, I had lunch with the singing star Kathryn Grayson, my dear friend Margaret Pereira, my secretary Debbie, and Dr. Maxine Asher. We dined at the famed Bistro Gardens in Beverly Hills. As we sat around, discussing this and that, the conversation turned to the world situation, something that happens often with my close friends.

I said, "I hate to read the front page of the newspaper these days because of all the problems in the world today. All I see are stories about rape, murder, gang warfare, dope, AIDS, political scandals, and pornography. It's so depressing."

Margaret asked, "Why can't the world change back to the way it was in the early 1900s? It was so innocent then. Is there a way to go forward on a higher spiritual level?"

Maxine answered, "What's going on today is not unusual. In every great period of history, when a radical change is about to occur, the world goes into chaos. It happened when Rome fell in 476 B.C. It occurred at the end of the Middle Ages. Things have to get worse before they get better. An ancient principle is that 'order comes out of chaos.'"

Then Debbie asked, "Maxine, you spoke about a great change. What do you mean?"

"I'm talking about the coming Age of Aquarius, which is the age of spiritual truth."

Kathryn, sitting opposite Margaret, looked a bit puzzled over Maxine's answer. She asked, "How does a person arrive at the Aquarian's spiritual truth?"

"By training the right side of the brain," Maxine said.

"Is there some scientific proof of this?" Kathryn inquired.

"Yes, some scientists are taking the 'brain revolution' quite seriously. In 1981, Dr. Roger Sperry of the California Institute of Technology won the Nobel Prize for proving that we have a left and right side of the brain. The right side has unique abilities when it comes to 'tuning in' to the spirit world."

"Like what?" Debbie asked.

"Like opening up to creativity, being intuitive, and also timeless."

"What does the left side do?" inquired Margaret.

"It is logical and rational; it also reads menus," I laughingly said. "Let's all read ours right now. I'm starved."

Maxine continued, "The right brain gives us information about the spirit world. We need to develop it for the purpose of reaching higher spiritual consciousness."

"Maxine," said Margaret, "is this mumbo-jumbo about the right brain actually true?"

"Yes, in fact more recent research was done by Dr. John Schwarz of Cal Tech University. He theorized there are many areas beyond the physical plane that humans can perceive. He calls his ideas the 'Superstring Theory.' In other words, when the physical earth was formed millions of years ago, other layers of invisible material were created at the same time, which vibrate faster than the earth itself. Sensitive people can perceive the existence of these higher dimensions and draw knowledge to themselves."

At this point, the waiter began tapping his foot impatiently. So we temporarily gave up our psychic conversation and concentrated on the appetizing variety of food listed on the menu. I was the first to order.

"I'll have fish — some orange roughy," I told the waiter.

"Not me," said Kathryn, "I'll have beef Stroganoff."

"Kathryn," I exclaimed, "You shouldn't eat red meat more than once a week. How about chicken or fish instead?"

"Ann, you're not serious," Kathryn laughed.

"Oh, yes I am. To keep my vitality intact, I don't smoke, drink hard liquor, or consume sugar and caffeine."

"C'mon Ann. I've known you for too long. You're not that pure," laughed Margaret.

"Well, I do like chocolate souffles, or a glass of wine with dinner. But, on the whole, I keep to a strict diet of green leafy vegetables, fruits, fish, and chicken most of the time. The brain and nervous system work better with good, simple food and, of course, the liver doesn't get overtaxed."

"The liver?" Debbie asked, "What's that got to do with it?"

"Well, in my discussions with doctors, I learned that the liver cleanses the toxins that come from using nervous energy. In order to keep the liver non-toxic, we must limit certain foods, like fats, sugar, caffeine, and alcohol. We also should drink eight glasses of purified water daily and have plenty of exercise."

By this time, the waiter was standing around listening to the conversation, trying to be polite, looking like he was ready to expire. "Ladies," he said tersely, "Please — have you made up your minds?"

"I've changed my mind," said Kathryn, "I'll have chicken curry."

"No, she won't," I told the waiter, "not with all that gravy. Bring her some broiled chicken instead." The waiter sighed and left in a huff.

"Are you telling me that broiled chicken will raise my spiritual awareness?" Kathryn said, laughing.

"No," I answered, "not by itself. You need to do many other things in order to increase your sensitivity." Then I explained about the people in Hunza, a country west of Pakistan, who live to over 100 years by eating simple foods. I also said that people in the ancient world ate natural foods and became robust and healthy. By paying attention to their diet, they accomplished wonderful things like engineering, math, and astronomy, as well as their reputed psychic talents. I also discussed the dietary habits of the Zen Buddhists who eat yin and yang foods for balance. Some of the yin foods are brown rice, whole wheat, nuts, and seeds. The yang foods include fruits, vegetables, and hot spices." I explained how diet helps the brain become sensitive to higher and higher wave lengths. The girls wanted to hear more, but by this time the food had arrived.

Between bites, Margaret commented, "It seems to me that training the brain is a full-time job. Does that include meditation, too, Ann?"

"Yes, it does, for some people. Lots of people meditate. I do, in my own way."

"What are the best ways to meditate?" Debbie asked.

"Every person probably has a different approach. Some use a crystal for concentration and some a candle in order to stare directly into the flame. Others sit on the floor in the Lotus position and close their eyes, or sit on the side of a mountain, or even in a green field. City people sometimes go into a closet and put a black bag over their heads to shut out the noise and light. I have never done any of this. Instead, I read a small book every morning called *The Daily Word*. Sometimes I read it at night before I go to sleep. It seems to bring me positive thoughts and clears away negative vibrations or irritations that have accumulated during the day. There are people who meditate to New Age music while others make the "OM" sound of the Zen Buddhists while meditating. To answer your question, there are dozens of different ways to meditate."

"I still don't see why it is necessary to meditate at all," Kathryn said.

"Yes, it is," Maxine protested. "For many people it is the only way they can clear their minds of negative energy." I said, "Exercise is the best way to do this. Dancing helps me."

"That I can understand," said Kathryn, choking down her plain broiled chicken.

"Some people also concentrate on color," Maxine continued, "Color is only a vibration on the electro-magnetic spectrum."

"Whoa!" said Margaret, "now you're going too fast for me."

"That's not complicated," said Debbie, "I learned about the electro-magnetic spectrum in a physics class. It measures color, sound, and other forces, like infra-red rays and light."

The girls were fascinated and had finished their entrees while listening. The waiter came by to ask if we wanted dessert. Despite the conversation about sugar, everyone ordered chocolate souffles, with whipped cream yet! When we finished, Margaret said, "Well, I've destroyed my mind for sure today." Everyone laughed.

I suggested we go back to my house for coffee — and talk some more. Fifteen minutes later, we gathered in the living room of my Beverly Hills home. Kathryn had taken out a pencil and paper. She said to Maxine, "I know you have written books and given lectures on developing the right brain. Can you give me a few suggestions in this area?"

"Well, I can't give you a 'how to' kit but I can offer a few ideas. For one thing, you can't rush the opening of the right side of the brain. It comes slowly. When you least expect it, you will observe a change in your awareness."

"What does that mean?" asked Debbie.

"Well, you might have valuable hunches, or even dreams that come true. You may also notice you are more creative."

"What else can we do?" Margaret asked.

"You must trust your dreams and hunches when they occur. For example, if Debbie has a dream that a handsome young man in a white Cadillac is going to come and propose marriage to her, she may become quite hopeful that this will happen right away. Then she waits days, months, or even years for the incident to occur but the man never appears. That's because the right brain is timeless. The dream could happen any 'time.' Do you see what I mean now?"

"You bet. I can't wait," whooped Debbie.

"You missed the point, Deb," chuckled Maxine.

"I've always been afraid of psychic things," confessed Margaret. It seems like witchcraft to me. You can open up the door to negative forces. Remember Ann's problems with the Ouija Board?"

Kathryn, who was taking in the conversation, appeared to be mesmerized. Debbie and Margaret knew all about my Ouija Board experience, so it didn't surprise them. Kathryn had been ignorant of the whole affair. Our short session grew into the evening hours.

"Can we continue this tomorrow?" they asked.

"Why not?" I said, "Be here at one o'clock." Then I had a thought. "Why don't you come for lunch? I'll make some steamed tofu, vegetables, and herb tea."

Kathryn winced, "I guess I can handle it," she said. "Anything for the good of my soul!"

The next day they came again, this time armed with notebooks.

"Please finish what you were saying yesterday, Maxine. Weren't there some more steps to follow?" asked Margaret.

"Just a few," Maxine said, "Learning to use the right brain is not a recipe. It's a way of life. For example, the brain gains greater awareness and experience through travel. If it is impossible to travel for physical reasons, or lack of funds, reading books about other countries will do almost the same thing. Keep the mind active. 'Use it or lose it.'"

I agreed with Maxine. I told the girls, "There's something else that's important. If you have a problem, there is a better way to solve it than through worry. The main thing is to release it to the universe and wait for the answer to come. 'Go with the flow.'"

Debbie said, "Annie—I *am* going with the flow, but my dream man hasn't shown up yet. I've waited all morning for the white Cadillac to pull up in front of our door."

"Oh, but it will," Maxine said gleefully, "when you least expect it. Just leave a space in your mind for it to happen. Don't think about it too much. Never force things. Be spontaneous."

Maxine continued, "Remember, Debbie, the human body is a sensitive and complicated organism. Ann and I always talk about

Oriental people and their belief in acupuncture, which balances body energy using needles to strengthen or sedate the meridians, or energy flows."

I said, "Some people have more powerful energy centers than others. In fact they actually attract electricity to them. I had an experience like that when I was nine years old. On the weekends, Mother and Dad would take me to visit my grandparents' home in Chireno, Texas. After a huge dinner of fried chicken, creamed gravy, and hot biscuits, Dad suggested we all take a walk. The evening was growing darker as we went down the lonely country road. I remember a hushed quality in the heavy, humid air. Everything seemed to stand still. The fireflies buzzed nervously around us as we ambled on and the night grew darker. Electricity was crackling in the air as a big storm was about to break. I was trailing a bit behind my parents, totally fascinated by the fireflies. Suddenly I had an uneasy feeling and turned to look behind me. There was a big fireball hovering in the air above me. It was about the size of a basketball. I yelled and Mom and Dad turned and saw it. As I ran back toward them, it followed me. When I stopped, it stopped. We all turned back and half ran toward the house. It followed along after us.

Dad stopped and said, "Don't be afraid. That's a fireball caused by the approaching electrical storm." It continued to hover near us and appeared to be watching us. Then it finally seemed to grow bored with this game and disappeared in a flash. I was nine years old at the time. I ran into the house, jumped into my bed and pulled the covers over me. The storm was about to break and I really felt the electricity in the air now. I knew it was going to be a big one, as the ominous thunder started rolling like drums in the distance. There was an open window by my bed. Directly across the room, another bay window also stood open. I was about to jump up to close them both when the big fireball came rolling through my bedside window, paused near my bed, and then went out the other window across the room in a flash. I was so stunned I started to cry. The fireball seemed to be taunting me. The storm finally broke and it poured. A voice said to me, "Leave it to the sky to cry, Lucille. Save your tears." I will never forget that experience. It will continue to haunt me for the rest of my life."

Margaret said "What an unusual story!"

I continued, "Speaking of electrical forces, I just read an article in the newspaper that demonstrates the power of electromagnetic energy and people's ability to attract it to them. A British housewife, Mrs. Pauline Shaw, knocked out 10 washing machines, 12 TV sets, 12 radios, 18 toasters, and 25 irons with her body, by barely touching the objects. She even broke a bank computer by leaning on the automatic teller terminal. I believe she probably could have done her housework by just raising her hand and moving everything into place. The power of her energy might have worked wonders for her if she had channeled it properly. Some people with a high energy field can physically wear down another person. Unless their energy is properly balanced in the body, the effect on people around them can be devastating. The receiver may become tired or even drained of his or her own energy. Individuals who take away energy are called 'psychic sappers.' At the end of an evening with them, you might feel totally 'wrung out,' like a wet dish rag."

After our discussion, the group met at my house a few more times to discuss other ways to increase mind awareness.

Maxine said, "The mind will open up a whole new world for you when it is properly developed. The right brain is like a miracle.

"Are we born that way?" asked Debbie.

"Yes," Maxine said, "We are all born with a highly developed right brain. Look how a baby moves toward colored objects placed over the crib (unless color-blind). The baby is also soothed by the mother's voice or by soft music. Unfortunately, the child soon has to cope with our physical world so he or she switches over to the left side of the brain in order to conform. Then the right side may close off, perhaps never to open again."

"When can we meet again?" the girls asked.

"Well," I said, "since you are now timeless and psychic, read my mind. Telepathy is a right brain skill. You should be able to tell when I want you to return, without my saying a thing." I laughed.

They walked out the door with a puzzled look.

"What's Ann talking about?" asked Margaret.

"Darn'd if I know," said Kathryn.

As I shut the door, I smiled to myself. I could see my friends had, at last, begun to travel down the long path toward higher spiritual awareness. I said to Debbie, "These ladies will be back soon for another session, I think Maxine and I have them hooked!"

CHAPTER XI.

Look to
the Stars

It is the stars,
The stars above us,
That govern our conditions.

WILLIAM SHAKESPEARE

Early in the 1980s, when I was playing in "Sugar Babies" in New York, the Iranian hostages chose our show as the first New York show they wanted to see after their release. Not long after, Ronald Reagan and his lovely first lady Nancy, who have been friends of mine in California for many years, also decided to make "Sugar Babies" the first show they saw after he became president. The audience was surprised and thrilled that night. They gave the Reagans a huge standing ovation. After the show, the President and his wife came backstage to meet the entire cast. The dancers and the orchestra were all "a-twitter," including Mickey and me. It was a truly happy event. Little did I dream that our president would later be shot, and that poor Nancy, who must at times have felt quite lonely as First Lady, would be attacked so viciously, over her interest in astrology by Don Regan in his book. Joan Quigley, in San Francisco, Nancy's personal astrologer, predicted the shooting of the president. Since then, Nancy has leaned more heavily on astrological predictions than she normally might have done at other times. Having known President Reagan, I don't think he would ever run our country by means of astrology. He's got too much good old "horse sense." Perhaps astrology gave Nancy a sense of comfort.

The astrologer Carroll Righter, who recently passed away, worked with many movie people. He held monthly parties for each astrological sign and all the important people in Hollywood came. He gave each of them an astrological nickname. Aries people like me were called "Hot Stuff Aries."

Anyone who uses astrology to predict events in his life should do the same thing I recommend for visiting a medium or clairvoyant. That is: put the data down on paper and tuck it away for future reference. Look at it now and then to see if any of the predictions have come true. If they have, you've had a great thrill. If not, you can throw it in the waste basket.

Many intuitive predictions actually have come true, depending on the ability of the psychic. Julius Caesar failed to heed the warning of his wife, Calpurnia, and the advice of his astrologers. He went to the Senate against their wishes on the "Ides of March" (March 15) and was murdered there. The ancients believed strongly in astrological predictions, and guided their lives by clairvoyance and intuition.

I have always been interested in astrology. My sun sign is Aries with Taurus as my rising sign. These are opposite configurations — fire and earth. I'm supposed to be full of vim, vigor, and vitality, as well as being a good politician. Aries is the sign of the ram. Aries people forge ahead, butting in where "angels fear to tread." My friends from MGM days, Debbie Reynolds and Janie Powell, are both Aries. Other stars like Joan Crawford, Bette Davis, Marlon Brando, and Charles Chaplin are Aries sun signs too. I've always said that Aries the Ram rhymes with "Ham," and I guess actors and actresses are a bit of that at times too.

There is a book called *Pursuit of Destiny*, which is out of print. It is the best beginner's book I have ever read on astrology. It gives the positive and negative side of each Zodiac symbol. It also explains what a balanced personality would be for each sign and shows a Tarot card representing the individual symbols at the bottom of the page. My card was "perfected work." I try to finish everything I start, even if it is not my best effort. I finish things to the "bloody end."

According to the Zodiac, there are twelve astrological signs. The Zodiac is an imaginary belt in the heavens, which includes the paths of the moon and all the principal planets. Its middle line is the ecliptic, or sun's path. These ancient signs were found on an early disk in the Temple of Dendera in Egypt. The unique artifact is now in Dusseldorf, Germany, having first been brought to Paris for exhibition at the time of its discovery, early in this century.

The twelve signs are represented by different symbols. For example, those born in August are Leo, the Lion; May is Taurus the Bull; June babies are Gemini the Twins; July is represented by Cancer, the Crab; November is Scorpio, the Scorpion, etc. The signs are also divided into four elements: fire, air, earth, and water. Astrologers believe that certain signs are more compatible with each other. For example, Aries and Leo are a good combination because they are both fire signs and fuel each other, unless they burn one other out. Aries and Pisces are fire and water. They might have a problem with their relationship, so astrologers say, because of a basic difference in personalities. In other words, the Pisces symbolically pours water on the Aries fire, putting out the flame. When Aries has an earth sign rising, like Taurus, Virgo, or Capricorn, they usually get along with all the other signs.

Of course astrology cannot make definitive statements about personality because it is not an exact science — other variables enter into human behavior, unrelated to the moon and stars. According to astrologers, everyone has a sun sign, a rising sign, a moon sign, and planetary signs, determined by plotting different elements on a chart. People's planets are also located at different points in the Zodiac, like Saturn, Uranus, Libra, or Pisces. Astrology, an ancient science, is quite complicated and people study the subject for years before they fully understand it.

One day I was gazing absentmindedly at the horoscope section of the daily paper when I said to Maxine: "Tell me, what is your sign?"

She answered, "I'm a Leo, Annie — a fire sign just like you. I also have Virgo rising, which is "earth," just like your Taurus rising. An astrologer told me I am full of vitality, but fortunately my Virgo earth rising sign keeps me practical. My moon is in Aries which gives me creative and artistic ability."

I replied, "I have my moon in Pisces which makes me psychic and a dreamer, as well as artistic and creative. Many famous people had their own personal astrologers — Woodrow Wilson, Mary Todd Lincoln, and others. It's not unusual to find well-known individuals throughout history who believed in astrological predictions.

"I learned the basis for astrology is the electro-magnetic pull the stars, moon, sun, and planets have on people's lives, based on their configurations in the heavens. The astrologer consults a book called an ephemeris, which tells him the location of the stars and planets on any given day in history. Since many events have occurred under so-called heavy planetary aspects, it is probable the energy given off during these times indirectly caused catastrophic events to occur. During a full moon, authors and psychics have theorized that more murders, heart attacks, and rapes occur. Sensitive people are vulnerable to such influences and so are animals. Coyotes, wolves, and other animals howl louder during a full moon. When there is an eclipse, or other cosmic abnormality, like a "blue moon" (two full moons in one month), people and animals often do bizarre things."

"Maybe that's where the werewolf legend developed!" Maxine

exclaimed.

"Very definitely," I answered, "We are vulnerable to cosmic forces. They can affect our health and well-being. For example, some people with arthritis feel pain before it rains because of a drop in barometric pressure. Of course that has nothing to do with the stars."

"What else do astrologers do?" asked Maxine.

"They are interested in the changing positions of the planets. For example, when the planet Mercury is "retrograde" (reversed), supposedly things tend to go awry. Communications become garbled, letters are lost in the mail, business deals fall through, and people are 'out of sorts.' Although it seems improbable that the heavens can create such havoc on earth, there have been repeated occurrences of such phenomena throughout history.

"Astronomy is the sister science of astrology. It has demonstrated the magnetic relationship of the planets to each other, and to the sun and earth. Magnetism keeps the planets in orbit. Sometimes, however, this magnetism weakens and a planet is temporarily pulled off its path. When this happens, many bizarre things can occur on earth, including weather changes, earthquakes, and other upheavals. The world's greatest catastrophes have occurred during such periods in history."

Maxine said, "Can you believe that relationships are sometimes governed by astrology? If Leo parents have a Scorpio son, they could have problems because Scorpio (water) and Leo (fire) are known to be incompatible signs. I know some people plan pregnancies so that their children will have the 'right' sign."

"That certainly is true," I told her. "My friend, actress Arlene Dahl, consulted her astrologer who picked the best day for her Caesarian section. The child, Lorenzo Lamas, famous as an actor on the TV show Falcon Crest, actually had his birth sign picked for him. People sometimes date and marry based on astrology. Businessmen make deals according to the stars. Skeptics claim the whole business is false because, over a period of time, the months have moved forward thirty days, except for leap year. This would mean the months accelerated by approximately thirty days, which would change Leo to Virgo, Virgo to Libra, etc. Astrologers answer their critics by saying that even with a thirty-day difference, the personalities and characteristics of each sign would basically be the same because they have not changed markedly in their position on the Zodiac.

"Some people cannot entertain the idea that they may not totally control their own destiny. They cannot believe we might be influenced by the God force. I believe mankind has a partnership with the universe as long as we stay in harmony with it. Astrology is an intuitive science that works to promote this harmonious relationship between us and the cosmos."

"Do you think that any scientific institutions believe in astrology?" Maxine asked.

"Not publicly, but I did read that NASA discovered its communication with outer space was interrupted when planetary energies went awry. At first they didn't know what was wrong. Planetary influences are very subtle. We can't actually see them, so we feel as if they don't exist. But their magnetic pull is there, and scientists are beginning to recognize it."

"What is the real purpose of astrology, Annie? I've been wondering about its meaning for a long time," Maxine asked.

"I believe that astrology is mathematical and scientific, attempting to plot events in advance to avoid catastrophe. It's like preventative medicine. It 'heads off' difficult times, or at least it has the potential to do this. It tells you about your good and bad days in a general way, even months and years."

"So many people are interested in astrology now. There seems to be a sudden resurgence of enthusiasm for an ancient science," Maxine added.

"Well, things are so unsettled at this time. People are restless. Astrology gives them a sense of comfort and reassurance. It is also a parlor game for some individuals. I recently heard someone say at a cocktail party, 'What's your sign?'

"I guess some people are tired of the question but others take it seriously. It is, however, a wonderful topic for casual conversation."

"Doesn't it take days to make an astrological chart?" Maxine asked.

"Not always. Astrologers now use computers. They can make a chart in minutes. But hand-done charts still take hours to complete."

"How much does it cost — I'd love to have one done."

"Most people cannot afford a hand-done chart. Computer charts can cost from ten to fifty dollars, but they're very general. Hand-done charts are more, perhaps as much as fifteen hundred dollars by the more famous astrologers, but you can get a good one for less. Much depends, too, on the ability of the individual astrologer to interpret the information in the chart."

"I don't know, Annie. I think I'd rather have a new dress," Maxine answered, laughing.

"The Egyptians and the Babylonians made star charts. The Greeks and the Romans used astrologers too. Even Charlemagne, in the Middle Ages, had his astrologer. Kings and Queens throughout history have consulted the heavens in order to make important decisions. Despite the criticism of Don Regan, astrology is a subject that people have always been interested in, including Nancy Reagan. Where there's smoke, there's fire. If so many people have used it for so long, it must be credible," I said.

"So what do the astrologers have to say to you, Annie?"

"I haven't had a chart made for many years but next week, I've invited a prominent astrologer to cast one for me."

"How long will it take?" Maxine asked.

"I'll give him the information, and it should take about a week to receive the finished chart."

"I can't wait to see it. Maybe I'll have one made too. We fire signs should stick together, Annie. I've heard that Leo and Aries have some wonderful things in store for them."

"I hope you're right. Only time will tell. After we have our charts interpreted, we'll write everything down and put the information in a drawer. Then, we'll look at it in six months to see if the information was correct. If not — so what? We had a lot of fun anyway!"

CHAPTER XII.

UFO's —
Fact
or Fiction?

The most beautiful thing we can experience is the mysterious. It is the source of all true art and science.

ALBERT EINSTEIN

All the newspapers around the world are talking about the "alien landing" in Moscow. The very conservative Russian news agency TASS spoke seriously about aliens claiming they were thirteen feet tall. Were the Russians putting us on , so to speak? Was the report a joke, or was it true? No one would believe the story if it were true because it's something perhaps only 'sensitives' take seriously or believe in. However, thousands of people around the world claim to have seen unidentified flying objects. Still others have read stories about UFO's and seen pictures, many of which have been blurred and unreliable. Although the existence of UFO's is highly questionable among skeptics, I have no doubt they exist, since I have seen them three times in my life and heard stories from many of my friends. Are UFO's fact or fiction? Read these accounts and decide for yourself.

When I was doing "Cactus Flower" in Dallas, Texas, I saw my first UFO. It was mid-afternoon when the sun was on the wane and the rays caught a silver disk moving through the sky. The object was not very high but it was close enough for me to realize it was not my imagination or an optical illusion. It hovered in the atmosphere for a minute or two and then took off so fast that I was mystified.

The second time I saw a UFO, I was in New York City, performing in "Sugar Babies." I was in my hotel suite at the Mayflower Hotel, which overlooked Central Park. The night was clear and cold and, around 4:00 a.m., I got up and went to my living room window to look out. There was a big white light in the sky that was so huge, it could not have been a planet or star. I called down to the front desk and all the hotel personnel went outside to see it. The next day, the newspapers said it was possibly a star or planet. Many people had called the paper because the light was so intensely bright. I, for one, saw it move away and stars don't move that fast. A UFO? I think it was.

When I was on tour with "Sugar Babies," it happened again. Debbie was outside on the balcony barbecuing a couple of steaks for the two of us, since I always eat my dinner after the show, due to the rigorous dancing I perform. We had a suite at the Residence Inn out in the country and the sky was very clear. There were only a few electric lights from the surrounding residential area, which were burning about 1:30 a.m. Debbie and I commented about how peaceful and quiet everything was when, all of a sudden, in the distance, we saw many lights criss-crossing and going up and down in a giant pattern. It looked like planes flying with demented pilots at the controls. It dawned on both Deb and me that no plane could go up and down and right and left at that intense speed. We saw the exact same display, at the same time, the following night. The next morning, after the second sighting, we called the Air Force who said they knew absolutely nothing about the occurrence. Later I learned from reading, and talking to other people, that the U.S. Air Force often withholds information they do not want released to the public. Yet, there is no doubt about what we saw on those two nights.

UFO's have captured people's imaginations for the past fifty years although ancient and medieval drawings show people looking up at strange objects in the heavens. The phenomenon has been reported in every country, with sightings primarily claimed in wide-open areas, at beaches, and on mountaintops. People have observed a variety of UFO shapes, ranging from long and tubular "cigar shaped" objects to oval, oblong, and diamond-shaped vehicles. Most UFO's give off an intense light, alternating in frequency, and tinged bright yellow or white. Some people claim to have seen UFO's with extraterrestrial beings in them who, according to reports, have taken earth citizens away in their space vehicles. The typical extraterrestrial is pictured as a large-headed creature with skinny legs and arms and big slanted eyes. I wondered whether these characters from outer space were fantasy like "ET" or real. To find out, I asked some very reliable friends of mine.

Astronaut Buzz Aldrin, his wife Lois Driggs, and I, had dinner together in Arizona. I asked him about UFO's, and if it was something the Air Force and the government was holding back from the public. He said he could not comment. In the *Blue Book of UFO Sightings,* editor Brad Steiger says that the United States government knew about UFO's in the fifties. Steiger claims the government tried to determine whether Martians or Russians dispatched the disks out into our atmosphere. This event happened shortly after World War II, when there was a great deal of confusion over the many sightings that were reported. With all the conflicting reports, no one knew what to believe.

Astronaut Edgar Mitchell is an advocate of the UFO theory and has spoken in favor of its scientific possibilities. He directs the Institute for Noetic Sciences, which studies metaphysical information. They have on record many UFO sightings. Here is one I heard first-hand:

White Indian trader Gordon Wheeler and his wife Lois, friends of mine from Sedona, told me some interesting stories about his personal experiences while living in Minot, North Dakota and working as a sergeant on the Minot Police Department. Gordon remembered a particularly quiet July night in the mid-1960s. While on duty as a special park force task officer, he had an unusual experience. In his own words, this is what happened:

"The evening was quiet and it was late. I decided to sit outside of my car and was watching the stars and just enjoying the beauty of the night. Out of the southwest, a greenish light appeared in the sky. It was small and at first I thought it was a plane. Then it started to move and I realized that no plane could move that fast and so quietly. There was absolutely no sound of engines and the speed with which it moved was unlike anything I had seen or heard before. It was heading toward the northeast. All of this lasted a total of five or six seconds. I was startled and hoped it would reappear so that I could confirm what I had seen. Sure enough, this light came back from the northeastern direction, heading in the same path back toward the southwest."

"And then what happened?" I asked him.

"At this point the object wasn't very high in the sky and I knew it was, without a doubt, a totally new encounter for me. It passed above me and continued on its path for another five seconds. Then it went up at about an 80x angle and powered right out of sight. In about three seconds, it was gone.

"On another evening in the summer of 1966, I was with my partner, Richard Meier, and we were on patrol. I remember the year because it was when the Ford Interceptor first came out and it was a very fast car. Minot, North Dakota, is circled on the south side by a bypass. I was looking toward the east as we were driving along and I saw this yellow fireball in the sky and it seemed to be hovering over the Northern States Power Company, an electrical station.

"What do you think it was?" I asked him.

"Well, Richard and I decided to drive over and see, so I floored the car and off we went. I guess we were going about 100 miles per hour and we turned on our red lights and tried to get to it. The road that we were on cut through three hills, and, as we entered each of the hills that were cut into the road, the fireball was momentarily lost from sight. Yet, as soon as we emerged, it was still there over the power plant. The total time needed to go through the three hills was 60 seconds at most. As we came closer, we noticed this thing about 60 to 70 feet above ground level. Richard and I used our spotlight, along with our red flashing lights, as we came nearer to the site. By the time we passed through the last hill, maybe a fifteen-second span of time, the object was gone. It seemed to be watching us, just as we were watching it."

"Did you report the happening?" I asked.

"Yes I did, and the next day I checked with a friend who worked for the power company and he told Richard and me that the night before, when we had observed this object, the company had lost several thousand kilowatt hours of electricity. They had no idea what had happened and, of course, there was no way to trace it."

"Was that the last time you saw UFO's in the area?" I questioned Gordon.

"No, it happened again in the same year, 1966, this time in the fall. We had still another unexplainable situation occur. A border patrolman was returning a prisoner from Portal, North Dakota, about five miles north of Burlington. Suddenly his car sputtered and just quit running. It just died and wouldn't restart. As he was trying to get it going again, he happened to look up to his left where there was a gentle slope to the land and saw a huge disk, about 60 feet in diameter, slowly descending down the hill at about 15 feet off the ground. It got to the bottom of the hill and set down on what looked to be a tripod. It stayed on the ground for about 30 seconds, then went back up the slope at the same speed and disappeared over the hill. This happened at about three in the afternoon and the border patrolman and his prisoner came to the Minot Police Department and told us what had just happened."

"Did the police do anything about it?" I asked.

"Yes, several of the officers including myself went out to the spot to investigate and what we found was incredible. There were several large rocks, about two to three feet in diameter that were turned over. Then there were several large boulders, about six to seven feet in diameter that were also turned over. It was as though they had been lifted up by some force and laid on their backs. We looked carefully for footprints on the ground but there were none. We looked at all the rocks and boulders for pry marks to see if something, or some machine, had moved them but we found not a mark on any of them. Even the dirt on the bottom of these rocks and boulders looked as if it had been lifted straight up out of the ground. Then we went to the place where the object had landed for a brief period of time and there were three marks on the ground. The amazing thing about this was the grass. It was absolutely white in the three marks where the tripod must have made contact with the ground. Being a policeman and doing investigative work for a living, we searched and searched for some signs to prove this had happened due to means that we could explain. We found nothing to explain the phenomenon."

After Gordon finished talking, I remembered seeing on television that there are reportedly hundreds of UFO landing sites around the world, distinguished by the nature of the dirt, which does not grow any living thing after a landing. These landing sites are in every continent and are believed to be used by outer space vehicles.

One impressive book on the subject is, *UFO's — Contact from the Pleiades.* Swiss adventurer Billy Meier took photographs of UFO's from high altitudes in the Alpine Mountains. His camera work was quite impressive and appears to be unretouched. In Los Angeles, a KABC talk show host investigated the Meier story and found it to be valid. The photographs showed various types and colors of UFO's, some at close range, displayed in a large, colorful book written about the sightings. Another account, the best selling *Communion,* recently published and now a movie, relates the story of one man's experience with extraterrestrials, a subject he never even thought about before the encounter. To prove his story authentic, the writer submitted to a lie detector test and had a psychiatrist certify he was not insane. He told the story many times on television. Unfortunately, no one but the author knows the real truth.

Most UFO sightings are reported by civilians rather than by the military. That is because if a military man reveals secrets about UFO's after his retirement, he can face a fine, imprisonment, or loss of his pension; possibly all three. Thus, it is easy to see why military sightings are so secretive.

J. Allen Hynek, a scientist and military man, has testified a number of times on the subject. He indicated our government has voluminous records about UFO landings, but will not make them public for fear people will become frightened. During the Eisenhower Administration, a UFO investigating committee was formed but nothing much happened as a result of that effort. Recently, Hynek's work was discussed on a television special, "UFO's Are Real." The film showed stacks of UFO reports and numerous government files on UFO's, which have been hidden or censored. It also gave testimony from former CIA chief, J. Edgar Hoover, and former president Jimmy Carter, both of whom have seen documentation on UFO's. In my opinion, the photographs of UFO's shown in the film were most convincing, but the question still remains — why is our government keeping the UFO question "under wraps?"

It seems to me we would be very shortsighted not to acknowledge the possibility of life on other planets and other universes. We must also realize that other cultures in outer space may already know how to evade time and space barriers. Thus, they are able to travel anywhere in the universe. Naturally, the physical appearance of UFO's would seem strange to us since they evolved from a totally different source; but their being here is a possibility. The SETI project, established by the United States in South America, set up huge radar screens to track signals from outer space. Various types of sounds were recorded at this site but are not translated because we do not understand the meaning of the signals coming to us.

What are UFO's? Basically, they are believed to be a form of high speed energy dispatched from anywhere in the universe which can move in any direction. A friend told me she saw a UFO on several different occasions. Each time she was with two other people and the group was astounded by what they saw. One sighting was at Malibu, California over the water. She was watching with two professors, one from Missouri and one from Texas. This sighting was at night when a round ball of light hovered over the horizon and then shot away straight upwards. The second sighting was at an afternoon garden party in Palm Desert, California. This time the UFO came within twenty feet of the spectators, one of whom was Bill Branch, a Las Vegas businessman. In both instances, the participants were looking in the same direction and saw the same thing.

In April 1988, another friend, Nancy Cook de Herrera, from Los Angeles, invited me and two other ladies to dinner at her home. I told them I was writing a chapter on UFO's for my book. I was amazed at the story Nancy told me. She said that in 1942, she was married and living in Honolulu, Hawaii with her husband, Lt. J. G. Dick Cook, of the prominent Cook family of Hawaii. Nancy herself is a well-known travel consultant, and I felt the story she related was absolutely true. She said she and her husband were invited to dinner at her sister-in-law's home. Commander Ralph Richardson was in charge of the submarine base in Honolulu. They had an Admiral of the Navy with them and the group went out on the lanai overlooking Diamond Head at dusk to have cocktails. Suddenly, over Diamond Head, hundreds of lights lit up the sky, streaking by so fast, it was mind boggling. Then the lights all shot straight up and disappeared. The entire group rushed into the house to phone the Naval Base but were told the sighting came up on the radar screens but no one knew what the signals meant. Nancy's husband called the Air Force and got the same answer. Could the Air Force and Navy have been afraid that a valid UFO sighting would alarm the public? It is a strong possibility.

Another UFO occurrence took place in New Mexico where a number of people testified they saw little men, less than four feet tall, with long arms and large heads. The event took place on a farm in the 1950s and the farmers actually tried to shoot the alien beings. Although the policeman later saw the marks from the shots on the wall, and heard a whooshing sound like a meteor, he could not find any evidence of a spaceship. Still, there were enough witnesses to that sighting to make anyone wonder what actually transpired.

Due to the vastness of space, UFO's could take thousands of years to arrive here on earth. Buzz Aldrin told me that in our current state of scientific development, it would take 200 years for an astronaut to reach Jupiter! So, you can see that time is relative when we deal with space. Author and researcher Dr. Egerton Sykes of Brighton, England, now deceased, believed that we have been watched by UFO's for over fifty years and that a space landing on our globe is imminent.

Do we need to fear such a landing? I don't think so. I believe that perhaps we can learn from space people. Hopefully they will play a role in unifying our planet, something we have not been able to do ourselves.

The UFO subject is very controversial but exciting. Even if you are a disbeliever, keep an open mind. Read extensively on the subject and study the night sky to see if you can detect anything. Do this over a long period of time. If you see what you believe to be a UFO, observe it without trying to take pictures. Don't run for your camera, telescope, etc., as this might disturb your "connection" to the object. Remember that as we travel with our eyes into the universe, time and space may slow down and the sighting may appear quite strange. In dealing with energy from other dimensions, you cannot force things to happen. They will occur on their own. Pilots have reported that their planes went out of control as they flew next to unidentified flying objects. The manner in which UFO's are propelled is believed to be totally different from our technology and incompatible with our own ways of thinking and reacting. Simply record your sightings in a diary. Try to feel, experience and observe what is happening, nothing more.

Some day interplanetary travel will be possible. I can hardly wait! Imagine the wonderful things one can see in outer space? I remember the comic strip character "Buck Rogers." He was a favorite with many people. Buck Rogers and Superman moved through space in ways that seemed totally ridiculous at the time they were published. Today, we take such space travel seriously. With the world now focused on outer space, and the shuttle Atlantis traversing the skies, we have finally reached the point where our awareness is open to such possibilities. Strange — my latest TV show is called "Out of this World," a sit-com about an alien — I find that quite amusing.

UFO's are probably propelled by force fields of energy beyond our wildest imaginations. Possibly some of them operate as fast as the speed of light. That does not, however, make them less real than an airplane or helicopter which operate in the physical plane. Of course, there is a prerequisite for acknowledging the existence of UFO's. First we must learn to live with our own planet. Then we may be ready for extraterrestrial life.

On the plains of Peru, there are drawings of giant spiders and other large animals, believed to be left by extraterrestrial beings who visited earth. These ancient astronauts needed a place to land their space vehicles and they created landing strips which are still visible today. The curator of these unusual designs is Maria Reiche, who has studied ancient space landings for decades. Peru is not the only country where we find evidence that ancient astronauts landed on earth. We also see proof in Mayan art and in the cave drawings of the Honduras. We think the drawings in Honduras represent an ancient astronaut in a space vehicle. It is more than coincidental that so many evidences of ancient space landings are found in this hemisphere.

I believe a person must, at times, allow his or her imagination to soar. What we think is a UFO may, of course, be a light from an airplane, a weather balloon, or a signal given off by aircraft or the military. Yet, unless we allow the possibilities of UFO's to come into our conscious mind, we will never recognize them. At least half of all sightings are probably misrepresented because people try to "force" the idea that they have seen something strange or different. However, a large majority of the sightings are real. When you do see one, you will know it. I have found my own experiences to be truly incredible.

CHAPTER XIII.

Ghosts and Apparitions

There must be ghosts all over the world.
They must be as countless as grains of the
sand, it seems to me.

HENRIK IBSEN

Ghosts! Who has not thought about these strange, ethereal apparitions? Tabloid magazines are filled with ghost sightings and reports of haunted houses. Many famous people claim to have seen ghosts, including author John Steinbeck, who viewed an apparition called, "Dark Watcher," on California's Monterey Peninsula. I have had several experiences with spirit presences — another name for ghosts. I know they exist and are merely in a non-physical form; departed beings who want to make themselves seen and heard again on earth.

In the 1960s, during my marriage to Arthur Cameron, Arthur took mother, Cobina Wright, the society columnist, and me to Lausanne, Switzerland, to visit the La Prairie Clinic of Dr. Paul Neihans. I was in my thirties, full of energy and in great health. Dr. Neihans gave shots to men and women seeking new vitality and youth. For the women he made injections of a liquid taken from cut-up lamb's glands. Naturally, I needed these shots like a hole in the head! Arthur, a multi-millionaire oil man, had read of Dr. Neihans and his rejuvenation formula, and felt he needed it. For men, the serum was taken from bull's glands and many men claimed it gave them a new lease on life — a more virile one. Charles Chaplin, Pope Pius, movie stars, and royalty had gone to the clinic. Now, it was my turn, and thanks to my husband, the "Cowardly Lion," I was talked into being the first to experience the benefits of the shots.

Arthur said, "Let Annie have the shots first. She is younger and, if it isn't too painful for her, we will take them."

I said, "Thanks a lot Arthur — you're making me your guinea pig!" But I did it out of love and respect for him.

Of course I was uneasy when I walked into Dr. Neihan's office at the La Prairie Clinic; but he was a tall, distinguished-looking man and very kind and gentle. We were assigned a room at the clinic and I prepared myself mentally to take the shots. The only thing that terrified me were the three large needles which did hurt when the doctor injected me with the serum. After two days I had no reaction, so Arthur, mother, and Cobina, took the shots too. Apparently I was overly optimistic, because I had a delayed reaction. After the two-day waiting period, I developed a high fever and wished I had never heard of Dr. Neihans or the La Prairie Clinic. Arthur was beginning to feel the same way but for different reasons. They allowed no liquor or smoking at the clinic, which was a big disappointment for him. They encouraged people to exercise, play golf and tennis, walk, and eat simple foods.

One night, Arthur asked one of the nurses to go and get him a bottle of bourbon. Being a Texan, he missed his cocktail before dinner. Somehow, with the right tip to the nurse, Arthur got his drink that evening. Then the lights were turned out and the time had come to go to sleep. A night light was plugged in across the room near the bathroom door, and a table and two chairs were against the wall. I was nearly asleep when I looked over toward the table and chairs and there sat a vision of my dear friend Bill O'Conner, laughing at the two of us. Bill had passed over a few years earlier and I was stunned at the apparition. I said, "Arthur — wake up and look across the room."

He did so, rubbing his eyes and said, "Isn't that Bill O'Conner? Annie — what is he doing here?" Then, while we both stared at the chair, Bill slowly faded away.

Bill and Arthur had been good friends. The shock of seeing his ghost was almost too much for him. After that night, Arthur abandoned his bourbon for the rest of his stay at La Prairie Clinic in Switzerland! We were both disturbed by the eerie event for weeks to come, yet we knew it had actually occurred, because we had both seen Bill sitting there that night in our room.

It is possible for spirit presences to appear and disappear in a matter of minutes or seconds. Usually, they only appear in physical form for a brief time and then return to the spirit world. In addition, not everyone can see them — only people who are "tuned in."

Hal Jacques, a reporter, told me that the actor Telly Savalas related this story to him. Apparently, Telly's car broke down on the road and he was standing, wondering what to do, when a man drove by and stopped. The man was wearing a white suit and asked Telly if he needed help. Telly said that he did and the man replied that there was a garage down the road. The man asked, "You need money, don't you? I'll loan you some."

160

Telly replied, "How did you know I needed money? I went out without my wallet." The man just smiled. He drove Telly to the garage where he got gasoline in a can and then he drove Telly back to his car. In gratitude, Telly said to the man, "I would like to call and thank you. May I please have your name and phone number?" The man wrote it down and left.

The next day Telly phoned the stranger's house to say thanks again. A woman answered. Telly said, "I'm Telly Savalas and I met your husband yesterday. I ran out of gas and he helped me."

She said, "What did he have on?"

"A white suit and shoes," answered Telly.

"Well," she said, "that's strange because I'm a widow. My husband died a year and a half ago and I buried him in a white suit and shoes." Telly was stunned. How do you account for this story? Was this man a ghost? Why did he appear at just that time to help Telly? This could have been a story for the "Twilight Zone."

Another friend from Los Angeles was traveling in New Brunswick, Canada. At 11:00 p.m., in a Howard Johnson's Hotel, she awoke to find an Indian, in full headdress, strangling her. She rang for the night manager. He came quickly but could find no one in the room. The next day she learned that the hotel had been built on the largest Indian burial ground in Canada. Inadvertently, she had "materialized" an Indian presence for a short period of time.

Is there any way to test such experiences? I think it is possible to find out, by polling sensitive people. I recently read of a study, funded by a grant from the National Institute for Mental Health. Researchers Richard A. Kalish and David K. Reynolds asked people of varied ethnic background in Los Angeles if they had ever experienced or felt the presence of anyone who had died. Forty-four percent of the people said they had. The researchers concluded that such contact is not delusional but is a valid personal reality and should not be discounted.

I asked Dr. Asher if she had ever experienced ghosts, and she told me a story that took place in a bed-and-board home in Ireland. These homes are out in the country and provide room and board for tourists who don't wish to have the expense of a hotel. She was the teacher and guide for a group of twenty-five people who had gone to Ireland. She was leading them to different archaeological sites. One night, Dr. Asher awoke with a start, clearly viewing hundreds of bloody bodies in front of her.

"What did you do?" I asked.

"Well," she replied, "I stared at them for a long time, not believing what I was viewing. Then I became very chilled and a bit sick to my stomach. I was fully awake at the time."

"Did they disappear?" I asked her.

"Yes, after about a minute but I had a difficult time getting back to sleep. Then, the next morning, I noticed that quite a few of my tour members were very quiet. I told them what had happened to me during the night. Six other people claimed they had the same experience. I was curious about what transpired so I asked the owner of the house for an explanation."

She said, "I'm not surprised, Dr. Asher. This house was built over an Irish battlefield that was used for hundreds of years. Many wars were fought here and many people died." Apparently, some sensitive members of Maxine's group picked up the same physical manifestation of the spirit presences on that site.

The group then went on to other parts of Ireland. Dr. Asher was invited to Castle Matrix in County Limerick, owned by Sean O'Driscoll. Sean planned a banquet in her honor, with many famous people in attendance, including author John Cohane, who wrote *The Key*. During the party, the host told the group that the castle was haunted because the Earl of Desmond had been murdered here. Just as he finished his words, all twelve of the high windows in the ancient dining room flew open at once. The guests gasped. Maxine shuddered. She thinks perhaps the ghost of the Earl heard what Sean said and wanted to make himself known to the group. And he certainly did!

After listening to her story, I told Maxine I was reminded of another ghost experience that happened to me in England. During my twelve years at MGM studios, I was sent out from time to time as a goodwill ambassador, and to make personal appearances with my movies. Even after my contract days were over, Ted Hatfield, of the International Press Department at the studio, called and asked if I would travel to London and Spain with their top foreign press representative Fred Sill. I accepted with pleasure. Fred was a tall attractive man with a great sense of humor and a student of history as well. We were to publicize "That's Entertainment I." MGM booked me into the Dorchester Hotel in Richard Burton and Liz Taylor's favorite corner suite with a great view of London and the boulevard below.

After my theater appearance, we came back to the hotel around

1:00 a.m. and I said goodnight to Fred and went to bed. Around 3:00 a.m., I was reading, and I heard voices in my living room speaking German, *loud* voices, the clinking of heels or boots and the clanking of glasses. I also heard the words, "Dumkopf" and "Haupstrasse" spoken several times. There was laughter too. I was puzzled and uneasy. I called downstairs to the night manager to come up as some people were in my living room talking loudly in German. I asked him how they got into the suite anyway. The phone rang later and he said, "Madame, there is no one there at the present time."

"But I distinctly heard them." I argued, "and I wasn't asleep. I've been awake reading."

"As I said, Madame, there is no one there now," he replied. I was quite frightened but somehow finally got back to sleep.

The next day Fred Sill came with the BBC-TV people to tape an interview in the Dorchester Suite, which is still beautiful though it is an old hotel. I told him what happened and he listened quietly. He said, "Well, Annie, in the early Forties, Nazi spies were all over London. In this hotel this was one of the suites they occupied." Then I told Fred I was psychic and I must have tuned in on energies from a long time ago. I couldn't think of any other explanation to clear up what had happened the night before.

Being psychic does not always bring happiness and can be very disturbing. That night I was quite alarmed when I heard the German voices. Even now, when I think about that evening, I get frightened all over again.

There are many books and writings devoted to ghost sightings which have appeared down through the ages. The ancients gave credence to ghost appearances, and Shakespeare wrote of Hamlet's ghost. Yet, these ideas were rejected by "rational" people who claimed the events were delusional, invented by man's mind. There have been reports of lights going on and off without an explanation, strange and mysterious noises, and apparitions of many forms and shapes. Sometimes a priest, or other religious leader, is called in to exorcise or even bless the area, as I had to do in my own home. Certain areas seem to be more prone to ghosts. For example, ghosts usually appear in isolated settings, in the country, or away from highly civilized areas. Secondly, it takes sensitive people to recognize them. Not everyone receives messages and sees apparitions from the spirit world. For most people, these things simply do not exist.

A friend of mine, Iris Schirmer, who was married to Rudolph Schirmer, the famous music publisher, does not normally think about ghosts. Yet, Iris told me this story. She was in Salzburg, Austria, and went to the home of Mozart. She entered the house and went up the stairs. Then she saw what appeared to be the figure of a woman on the first landing. On the second landing she saw the same thing. Confused and a bit frightened by the apparition, she told someone what she had seen. It turned out that the description she gave fit that of Mozart's mother. Other people had reportedly seen the same apparition in times past. Iris was shocked by the experience.

In 1980, during the run of "Sugar Babies" in New York City, Debbie and I frequently packed up the dogs and drove to Buck's County, Pennsylvania on our weekend off. It was about a two-and-a-half hour drive from the city. At one time Buck's County was a mecca for performers and wealthy people from the New York area who came there to relax and rest after their busy lives in the "Big Apple." Buck's County is also famous for its antique stores. The long drive was well worth it, as one entered this beautiful area. We stayed at the Center Bridge Inn which was on the canal and the Delaware River. It was used in the 1700s as a Lock House and they lowered or raised the bridges for the busy traffic of the ships and boats on the mighty Delaware. I rented a lovely two-bedroom suite with a living room, and a view off the porch of the river and the trees. I could also open the living room doors and sit by the old fireplace, looking down the hall, where guests came and went to the rooms upstairs, and the pub and restaurant down below. The rooms were all done in Victorian-style decor.

One Sunday night we arrived around 1:00 a.m. It was raining and I knocked on the door until the owner, a young man in his twenties, let us in. We tiptoed down the hall so as not to disturb the other guests as it was so late. He helped us with our bags and we were chatting quietly in the living room. I looked over the owner's shoulder and saw another young man with reddish hair, a tan pin-striped suit, high stiff white collar, and tan high button shoes. He went through the front door and up the stairs to the rooms. He looked very Victorian. I said, "Who was the gentleman who just came in?"

The owner said, "Oh, I've locked up for the night, Miss Miller, no one can come in now."

"I beg your pardon sir," I answered, "but a young man just came in and went up the stairs."

"That's impossible," he protested, "no one is in the inn tonight except for you and your secretary, and myself. All the weekend guests go home on Sunday night." Needless to say, I didn't sleep too well that night or the next night, despite the beauty of the hotel. Eventually I rented a small house in Lumberville down the road, overlooking the canal and the Delaware River, and was at peace again. The entire area was rather haunted, as many men had been killed there in the Revolutionary War. Washington crossed the Delaware not much farther down the road.

Ghost sightings almost always occur to sensitive people. Although ghosts and poltergeists are only energy in a non-physical form, they seem frightening because they are not part of our rational world. We are accustomed to experiencing everything through our senses. When something comes into our reality structure that is totally new to our experience, the event can be alarming. Still, ghosts and apparitions must be accounted for, because they are part of psychic phenomena, coming from dimensions that are completely unknown.

The next story is not a ghost story but it happened to me and was both frightening and true. An evil presence or energy can emanate from a living being. I experienced this occurrence when I was invited to a ranch in Ojai, California as the guest of a beautiful young heiress. When I arrived, I met and shook hands with a doctor of psychiatry who was her date for the weekend. Immediately, I felt a resentment toward this man and I sensed that he felt the same way about me too. Was this karmic? My friend, the heiress, was dating him so I took her aside and said, "Please be careful. There is something rather devious about your date. Don't get serious over him."

She laughed and said, "Thanks, Annie. I'll try and heed your advice."

I sensed he was cold and calculating and mainly after her money, even though she was a beautiful and charming woman. After dinner, I said goodnight and went to my room to relax and read. I locked the doors and windows to my room, since I was on the ground floor and felt uneasy. I was reading a book in bed when suddenly I felt hands upon my throat, strangling me. I choked, screamed, and fought against the force. I was in such a frenzy that I even hit the lamp during this struggle and it fell over. I heard people rapping on my door who had come to help me. When I opened it, they came in but nothing was there except bruises on my throat. As I look back on this experience, I believe it can be explained. Physically I must have picked up his energy. The man who disliked me so intensely must have projected his mind and evil presence into my room to warn me not to interfere with his devious plans to try to marry my friend. I'll never forget this strange experience. Incidentally, she took my advice and didn't marry him, but married someone else instead.

The appearance of ghosts are real occurrences to some people. When ghosts come into our realm, it is usually to warn us, help us, or sometimes to annoy us — but they should not be discounted or taken lightly. After all, ghosts are a very real part of the psychic and spiritual world.

CHAPTER XIV.

Universal Mind

Despite the fact that the psychic world is mysterious as well as instructional, there are serious aspects to its use. We are on the edge of world revolution. This time the challenge will be the changing of world consciousness, not concentration on atomic warfare. Our problems today deal with pollution, drug addiction, incurable illness, and declining morals. The value system set down by our ancestors has been replaced by an era of "no values," where "anything goes." Millions of people are indolent and shiftless, driven by purely selfish concerns, like money, power, and sex. These goals are not new to civilized man. They have always been around. However, religion, values, and morals have usually balanced selfish needs. For many who want to stay with the old ways, these are terrible times in which to live. What, if anything, can be done about it?

One world leader who made a marked change in world consciousness is President Gorbachev of the Soviet Union. In 1989, he finally convinced his colleagues to give religious freedom to the people, while also loosening the Marxist hold on Eastern Europe and allowing the destruction of the Berlin Wall. Then Gorbachev visited the Vatican for the first time in several decades, inviting the Pope to come to Russia. These steps, and the reactivation of the Russian Orthodox Church, are a major step forward in the world today.

I believe our declining morals have resulted from a blocking of people's awareness, turning it away from the spiritual world. There is a shield of heavy vibrations covering the earth plane, preventing contact with the God force, the positive energy of the universe, within and without. When people are inundated with negativity, they unwittingly use energy improperly. Such misuse of energy systematically destroys the planet. History tells of other such epochs: the end of Atlantis, the fall of the Roman Empire, the decline of the Middle Ages, and the French and Russian Revolutions. These are just a few such periods in the long story of man's record on earth.

If used properly, the power of mind may save us all. The positive energy of the God-force has unlimited potential. Turned against itself, it can be a dangerous and a destructive weapon.

One of the world's biggest problems today is ecological. We have upset the balance of nature by systematically polluting the air, our water supply, and the planet. Adding to the problems, the world is getting warmer, due to the Greenhouse Effect, where hot air is trapped by the atmosphere. The problem is not related to the natural order of things. It deals with man's consciousness, and his neglect of the global environment. For example, the huge oil spills destroying the oceans and wildlife. The Great Lakes are polluted and drying up. The North Sea is decaying and eventually will not sustain fish or sea life of any kind. The oceans are filled with trash, and more recently, with syringes and blood samples from AIDS patients, posing an immediate threat to life itself. This is a great tragedy since the oceans are the lungs of our planet. Our waterways are treacherous places, threatening drinking water and basic hygiene.

The air we breathe is thick with chemicals. The pollution in Los Angeles has turned the sky gray and even the national parks are threatened. People are developing breathing problems at a horrifying rate. Pollution has entered our office buildings, especially those without windows. Air conditioning units are filled with toxic wastes. It is unsafe to breathe or drink tap water. If people had realized what might have happened twenty years ago, we might have forestalled the disaster. Little attention was paid to people like Barry Commoner, who wrote *The Closing Circle,* and other advocates of clean environment. Everyone thought pollution would never spread, so they allowed things to get worse. Most of us figured "the other guy would do it." Unfortunately, that never happened. Now people everywhere have no choice but to band together in consciousness, taking action to make a change. There is so little time and so much must be done.

Basically, the world's problems cannot be solved through a purely physical approach. Shutting down car exhausts and factories is a small "stop gap" measure that has little value, like putting in a cork to stop a leak in a dike. There is only one answer: raising global consciousness to the point where people will not *want* to pollute and will think critically every time they are tempted to do so. All of us must concentrate on improving our inter-relationships with our fellow humans. Every action we take and every word we utter, has a direct effect on the world community. We do not live in isolation as we did in days gone by. We must learn to live together or we will die together.

Our "ME" generation dwells only on physical satisfaction. As such, it is destined to destroy itself in short order. Perhaps another savior is needed — someone who, like Jesus, comes to earth during a dark period in man's history, bringing salvation and light to a troubled world. I believe such a "second coming" may occur, but first people everywhere must make a spiritual change, sacrificing their personal gains for the greater good of mankind.

Another requirement for saving the planet is the slowing down of the pace — moving out of the fast lane and regrouping on saner foundations. When a society accelerates as rapidly as our own, morals and manners are abandoned. The "chase" becomes more important than the goal. Ultimately, if one doesn't focus on direction, the final destination turns out to be disastrous. In fact, the path we've taken now may result in a horror story beyond our wildest imagination.

Goals and objectives are critical for any advancing society. One cannot just "do one's own thing" without regard for the ultimate end. That is hedonism at its height.

For example, space travel is a wonderful thing. Yet we have ruined outer space by leaving debris in the atmosphere and on the moon. Our civilization has left its damaging mark everywhere.

The minds of our youth are distorted because we have allowed drugs into the culture, causing an entire generation to "space out," unaware of what is really going on. The media is partly responsible. Films are getting better, but a recent movie such as "Colors" glorifies profane language, killings, gang warfare, and narcotics. There is less desire for legitimate drama today. Thank God for movies like "Driving Miss Daisy," which won the 1989 Academy Award. People are weary of nudity, violence, and four-letter words."

Gangs roam the streets of our cities, yet who could blame the young people who frequent them? With no family structure, and no place to go, gangs are reasonable alternatives to emotional survival for many of our youth. Drive-by killings? They happen every day in our major urban centers. Do anything for excitement. That was the motto of the Eighties.

For some Christians, belief in God, and a strict attention to the Ten Commandments go a long way toward curbing this trend. Helping people understand universal law will also assist young and old alike. Equalizing society, making sure the poor receive the aid they need, is also critical. Who can think of global concerns when hunger is such a pressing factor?

Schools must start mind training, concentrating on inquiry and critical thinking. Education must foster creativity and teach world awareness. It is better to learn about pollution than basketball, more important to find out about AIDS, than making tissue paper puppets for a festival. Let's get down to the basic needs of society with our youth, who can still do something about the world we live in.

Every profession must seek alternative answers. Organized medicine should give a serious nod to holistic healing, to find a common ground for curing disease. Law must balance its tenets to reflect the needs of the earth and humanity, as well as the individual. Even engineers and architects need to concentrate on the human factor in the structures they design.

In a sense, we are all related, occupying the same planet, tuning into the same spiritual reality, and dealing with the same universal energy. What we do with these factors determines whether the human race will survive. If we do not change, we will destroy ourselves, and that is the worst of all alternatives. That is why I am concerned, and one of the main reasons I decided to write this book.

I believe global disaster can be forestalled if spiritual wisdom is recognized, as a way of gaining higher awareness. When the human race grasps new dimensions of being, it may find a means to save the planet. By tapping into the force, human beings will be guaranteed a greater degree of wisdom and the power to make the necessary changes.

The native American people have always known how to balance the energy of the universe. They lived in harmony with nature and took responsibility for their actions. Today we can learn from Indian wisdom. The following statement from Chief Seattle to President Franklin Pierce in 1855, entitled "Where is the Eagle Gone," was an early warning to the white man about the consequences of polluting the environment:

> The Great Chief in Washington sends word that he wishes to buy our land. How can you buy or sell the sky — the warmth of the land; the idea is strange to us.
>
> Yet we do not own the freshness of the air or the sparkle of the water. How can you buy them from us? Every part of this earth is sacred to my people.

We know that white man does not understand our ways. One portion of the land is the same to him as the next, for he is a stranger who comes in the night and takes from the land whatever he needs. The earth is not his brother but his enemy, and when he has conquered it, he moves on. He leaves his father's graves and his children's birthright is forgotten.

There is no quiet place in the white man's cities. No place to hear the leaves of spring or the rustle of insect wings. But perhaps because I am savage and do not understand — the clatter only seems to insult the ears. And what is there to life if a man cannot hear the lovely cry of the whippoorwill or the arguments of the frog around the pond at night.

The whites too, shall pass — perhaps sooner than other tribes. Continue to contaminate your bed and you will one night suffocate in your own waste. When the buffalo are all slaughtered, the wild horses all tamed, the secret corners of the forest heavy with the scent of many men, and the view of the ripe hills blotted by talking wires. Where is the thicket? — GONE — where is the eagle? — HE HAS GONE — good bye to the swift and the hunt, the end of living and beginning of survival.

CHAPTER XV.

Other Realms of the Psychic World

*Many are in high places and of renown, but
mysteries are revealed unto the meek.*

THE HOLY BIBLE

Other countries have investigated extra-sensory perception for years. The United States is a latecomer to the field. In 1988, a U.S. Senator from Rhode Island first expressed serious interest in the "force." Senator Claiborne Pell stated that he would spend more time investigating psychic research because, "I have always been intellectually curious, and I think these things should be examined…I would like to see more emphasis placed on developing human intuition and human potential because many times theories that seem ridiculous at the time produce greater areas of knowledge." Senator Pell's statement is a giant step toward public recognition of the metaphysical field. He is to be commended for his forthright statements.

One important area of psychic investigation is auras, a phenomenon that has always puzzled me. Auras are energy fields which surround every living being, including plants. Some people see them frequently, often in a variety of colors. I am not able to do so, but people have observed them around me. Recently, I went into a department store to look for a new perfume and the lady who helped me was from Sweden.

She said, "Miss Miller, I can see your aura. It has blue, purple, yellow, and orange in it. That means you are a very spiritual person and very psychic, aren't you?"

I said, "Yes I am. Thank you." Her words startled me, as I've never known anyone who could "see" my energy field.

The aura of each person depends on his individual capacity to transmit the life force. The stronger the energy is generated within each person, the larger the aura extends out of the body. According to reports from metaphysicians, the color of the aura determines where each person is "coming from." Thus, a red aura would mean that the person is at a lower physical vibration than someone who projects purple. Auras change within each person, depending on individual circumstances. The aura of a sick person might be short and thin. A well person, full of buoyant energy, would have a thick, full vibration surrounding him. Each organ of the body has its own individual pattern. It is believed that, when this aura is broken, the organ becomes diseased.

The aura of one person can be damaged by the vibrations of another, if that person sends energy that is strongly incompatible with the other person's force field. Auras protect us in a psychic way. Once the aura is broken, it is necessary for an individual to go to a quiet place to restore himself, using meditation, solitude, or whatever method is beneficial, based on previous experience. Psychic people often enjoy being alone at times, because it keeps their aura intact.

Recently, Russian research discovered that the aura can be photographed by a process developed by Semyon Kirlian. The technique, called Kirlian photography, is different from ordinary picture-taking, since it uses a process that measures electro-magnetic energy emanating from an object or person. To measure a person's energy field, the subject puts his thumb, or a hand, on a metal plate and the photography begins. The picture comes out in reds and blues, with a white glowing area surrounding the object, which is the aura. Dying plants have a fragile aura, healthy ones a thick ring around them. People who have expended energy just before taking a photograph produce a thin aura. I asked Maxine if she had ever seen Kirlian photography. She showed me some colored photographs. I said, "Where did you get these?"

She replied, "They were made by Dr. Harold Vogt in Wichita, Kansas. I saw him use the Kirlian process on people 'in love.' The size of their auras was enormous."

I told Maxine that Adele Tinning, the psychic from San Diego, who uses a kitchen table for her mediumship activities, has photographs of auras around her hands and head. She also has photographs of some of her subjects with auras around their bodies too.

I asked Maxine, "Can you also 'feel' auras?"

"In a sense you can, Annie. When you are tired and depleted from dancing, or some other activity, you can be sure your aura is greatly diminished as well. It all has to do with the nervous system which tires easily. Nerves take longer to regenerate than any other organ in the body. That's why we must alternate work with rest in everything we do."

I pondered what she said and then I asked her. "I've read that people can have an out-of-body experience. Is that related to the aura?"

"No. An out-of-body experience occurs when the soul is at a high spiritual level — a high rate of vibration. When that happens, the soul can actually leave the physical body and float upward. However, it usually always returns."

"What do you mean — usually? Is there a danger of it not returning?"

"Well, metaphysicians believe that a silver cord connects the body to its spiritual essence. If, for some reason, that cord becomes broken during an out-of-body experience, the person could die." I told Maxine about Shirley MacLaine's TV movie, "Out on a Limb." It had a great scene in it showing the attachment of the silver cord to the soul as it left the sleeping body.

Some Christians believe that Jesus could astral-project, meaning his spiritual vibration could travel anywhere in the world. This is a form of out-of-body experience. In some accounts, it was reported that Jesus appeared to people in India and other countries far away from Palestine.

Then I said, "Let's talk about psychometry. I saw Peter Hurkos psychometrize objects. It was amazing."

"You mean holding or touching an object and intuitively gaining information about it?"

"Yes, that's exactly what I mean."

Maxine said, "I saw some incredible dowsing at Cashan, Arizona near Phoenix. Bill Cox, an expert dowser, took an Indian artifact and, after using psychometry, held it to his chest and gave a 'reading'. When Bill was through, an Indian expert told him he was absolutely correct. Then I read that in Canada, many different psychics were given artifacts to psychometrize. In almost every instance, they gave the same information about the object."

"Maxine, Peter Hurkos was an expert in psychometry. He solved the 'Boston Strangler' murder case by holding objects used by the 'Strangler' which, along with ESP, gave him valuable information about the case."

"Are there any recent experiments with ESP?" I asked her.

"Only the work done by the Rhines on 'probability,' at Duke University, and the outstanding research conducted by Dr. Thelma Moss at U.C.L.A. Dr. Moss had people communicating telepathically over distances of more than 6,000 miles."

"I haven't read about any recent experiments."

"I think it's because telepathy is now well accepted, even among skeptical scientists. Almost everyone has had a telepathic experience. You can read another person's mind, or guess what they're going to say, before they actually say it. That's a common occurrence, especially between people who know each other well, like you and Debbie."

Maxine continued, "What is hearing beyond the normal range, Annie? I just saw the film "Field of Dreams," where a man heard a voice which led him to build a baseball field in a pasture. Do you think that is possible?"

"Very definitely," I answered. "Extended hearing simply means clair-audience, perceiving beyond the normal range, tapping into another dimension. Several years ago, I had an emotional experience which also was extrasensory. My mother was lying in a hospital, hovering between life and death. I had no idea if she would pull through, as she was in a semi-conscious state. I took a pencil and put it down on a piece of paper and asked, "Is Mother going to make it?" The pencil spelled out the word "yes," without my consciously moving it. Shortly afterward, Mother pulled through. Her first words were, "Hello, baby." Later I learned that encounters like that are called automatic writing.

Maxine looked at me with great interest when she heard the words "automatic writing." She answered, "During my archaeological investigations, I had similar experiences in caves, tombs, and at ancient sites. Other scientists, friends of mine, like Dr. Egerton Sykes, reported the same experience. Information simply channeled through them onto the pages of their diaries or report books. This information sometimes took the form of facts they had never learned or studied at previous times. For example, if you stand at Stonehenge, or at the Parthenon, or at the pyramids of Egypt, you may suddenly have insight into an earlier civilization you know nothing about. Knowledge is a form of energy. Sensitive, right-brain-dominant people may subconsciously pick up this information. People sometimes write entire books about subjects they only know in a general way. The facts channel through them onto the printed page."

"Is that like the Taylor Caldwell experience?"

"Exactly," Maxine answered. "Many historical novels are written by people who subconsciously 'know' all about their subject without having studied it."

"Yes, I know. There are other things I'd like to know more about — like tarot cards. When I was in New York, Arlene Dahl gave me a set for my birthday and said they could predict the future. I thought they were interesting but I didn't know how to use them. Still, they looked like a game that could be fun.

"Arlene said, 'It's not a game, Annie — it's a serious subject for me and for the people who use the cards'.

" 'Serious — in what way?' I asked her.

" 'The tarot gives predictions to people about their lives. The cards are printed with symbols. Each symbol has a special meaning. The tarot reader learns to interpret their significance by using psychic skills. Tarot cards are very ancient."

" 'Well,' I said, "I know that the ancients wrote their languages symbolically but I didn't know about the cards'.

"Arlene said, 'It's another form of psychic concentration. I've written quite a few books on astrology and the tarot, which were very successful. I'll bring them over to you'. I thanked Arlene and left."

Later I learned from psychics that when the Library at Alexandria was destroyed in 394 B.C., the knowledge in it was committed to symbols by the people who memorized the ancient books. Later these symbols became the basis for the tarot.

Maxine said, "Another thing I'm curious about, Annie, is the subject of trances."

"Trances are a semi-conscious state, Maxine, like the feeling you have just before you fall asleep."

"Yes, I do know that feeling but I'm curious about whether people who write vividly about the ancient world are in a trance state when they do it."

"I think so, Maxine. Many great authors have written in a semi-trance state. Mary Renault, who wrote *The King Must Die, The Last of the Wine,* and *Alexander the Great,* must have been in a hypnotic state, since she wrote about Greece in such a colorful way. You can smell the blood of the bulls and see the bull dancers. You can taste the dust, visualize the blue of the sea and the whiteness of the temples. You can even hear the music of the lutes. Joan Grant and Evelyn Wells wrote about Egypt as if they were born there. Evelyn Wells wrote of Cleopatra and Hatshepsut as if they were her blood sisters. Joan Grant wrote vividly of ancient Egypt and the love stories of Italy and Greece."

Maxine said, "That's very interesting — any others?"

"Yes, there are more. Lawrence Durell wrote Justine which takes place in the Middle East and the Casbahs. When I read his books, I can smell jasmine, see the marketplaces, smell the camel and donkey dung and the urine of the peasant children in the medinas. M. M. Kaye wrote *Far Pavilions*, a story of India, which also showed 'far memory,' since she wrote so vividly about the people. Jess Stearn, a disbeliever of psychic phenomena and a tough news reporter when he started, became a believer in this kind of 'knowing' when he wrote about the great seer, Edgar Cayce. He told me he became psychic himself and opened up his 'third eye' after working with psychic people."

"How do people get into a trance, Annie?"

"It can be self-induced or done under hypnosis by another person. The musical, 'On a Clear Day You Can See Forever,' shows this kind of hypnosis. The film was done well. The problem with trances is that a medium, in the trance state, could die if awakened while she is still 'under'. Someone should always be there with her. If a person goes under hypnosis to stop a bad habit like drinking or smoking, they should go to a well-known doctor of hypnosis. During a trance, the heartbeat slows down, the breathing is slight, and the eyes may or may not be opened. If the person awakens normally, all goes well."

"I'm fascinated," Maxine said. "Now tell me something about handwriting analysis. Do you know anything about it?"

"I write in a large script which means I 'think big' and am very creative and artistic. Each type of writing means something different to the analyst who interprets the meaning for his client. Handwriting analysts use scientific methods to measure the size, shape, slant, and configuration of the writing. Then they psychically interpret its meaning. Palmistry is somewhat the same except that the palmist reads the lines and creases on the hand. I have had my palm read many times. I have a long life-line and a strong heart-line, among other things. Palmistry is a very ancient art. Each line and crease is plotted, just like a road map. Palmists compare thousands of these 'maps' before making their interpretations.

"Numerology is interesting too. The numbers and their meanings can determine the future for some people. Three and six are said to be spiritual numbers. Each number has its own symbolic interpretation. Although mathematics is said to be a rational science, it is actually based on the interpretation of symbols. This is especially true of higher math like calculus."

Maxine said, "I only wish I was good enough at math to win the

California or Arizona lotteries." We both laughed.

"What about the kinds of psychic behavior that seem to be evil — like witchcraft, omens, and spells?" I answered Maxine by saying that I did not deal with these subjects. In my opinion, they are the dark forces and I will not meddle in that area. I explained to her about devil worship, which is so prevalent around our country and that I have never had anything to do with negative experiences. There are many kinds of metaphysical phenomena. It is important to use your psychic energy wisely and in a positive way.

CHAPTER XVI.

Tapping into the Force

Train your mind while your brain is still alive. When your brain dies, your mind energy will live on forever.

DR. WILDER ENFIELD

This book has spanned a horizon of subjects from auras to UFO's, including ways to contact the spirit world. The final subject deals with ways to open the "third eye," leading to greater awareness about the infinite mind. If you are a sensitive, you probably already know the steps to follow. If not, I would like to express ways in which I open and maintain the psychic and spiritual centers of my mind.

1. Go to a quiet place away from loved ones, children, and pets. The back yard, your car, a spare room, or the beach are excellent places to retreat.

2. Relax your mind and body. Try to forget everyday worries. Clear your consciousness of all distracting thoughts.

3. Play soft music, without lyrics, if music makes you relax.

4. Be still and listen to your inner mind. Close your eyes but try not to fall asleep.

5. Silently ask God to help you. Visualize a white light around you to keep out negative forces.

6. If you are troubled and need help, hold a pad and pencil. As you contact the spirit world, the answer may come through automatic writing.

7. You can also make contact with the spirit world by concentrating on an object, a flower, or a lighted candle.

8. Somehow, in time, the answer you seek will be given to you. You will know when this happens. Be patient. It may take considerable effort before the answer comes to you. Recognize that the spirit world is a reality located in a different plane of existence. Once you believe in that possibility, spirit will come to you sooner. The universe answers all of our prayers, if we don't block them with negative thoughts. If you want to find out if a loved one, who has passed over, is at peace in another plane of existence, ask in God's name. Hold an object that belonged to that person. In time, the answer will come.

I believe you must practice these steps only when you are troubled. Observe the unfolding of your psychic force a little at a time. Let things happen slowly. The mind is like a radio receiving set. You might get static at first but eventually the channel will clear. It takes time, and a large degree of dedication, for most people to open up their "third eye" and for the subconscious mind to grow strong.

Meditate daily. This clears the mind of excess energy and gives you a clearer view of the day's problems facing you. Listen to your inner voice or your hunches. It could be your guardian angel looking over you. Diet is important to increase your psychic energy (as we have discussed earlier in this book). The same is true of exercise. Go for a walk and tune into nature and the universe to clear your mind. Remember, only contact the spirit world in case of a problem, or if you have something very important to resolve.

Be happy. Don't take life too seriously. If you can afford to travel, go camping or fishing. Buy travel books that show you pictures of far away places. These activities will clear your mind and help you relax and tune into the universe. Believe in the principle of divine order. This means everything is happening for your greater good even if it doesn't seem so at the time. When you have an intuition or a dream, write it down and follow it. Keep away from people, including family members, who upset or drain you. If this is not possible, find a quiet place, even in the bathroom, to pull down your mental shade. Retreat from the noise and upset of life at least once daily. It is food for the brain.

Much of the above is drawn from the customs and the practices of ancient people who were more in tune with the universe than our present generation. The ancients practiced meditation, proper diet, and proper thinking. They worked and played in harmony with nature. We can all benefit from their example.

For instance, before a performance on stage, I always ask my dresser, hairdresser, and secretary to leave my dressing room so I can be alone. They usually ask me why since they enjoy watching a small television set in the area where I make up for the show. "Please don't be offended," I say, "because I gather all my energies and my force-field around me by sitting and meditating and calling on the good forces to give me strength and power for a strong performance." So many people ask, "Isn't it hard, day after day and night after night, to go out on stage and do the same show? Don't you get bored?" I always answer "No, each time is like `opening night' to me." I contact people with all the electrical currents my body can produce and using my power of mind, overcoming any aches or pains or flu bugs my body might have, then I do the show to the best of my ability. To do this, I relax and let the power of the universe come in. In other words, I "Tap into the Force"!

EPILOGUE

It is now eight months since "Sugar Babies" closed in London. I'm back home, in the Beverly Hills house I inherited from my mother upon her death. It's a home where I feel happy and secure. It's my "Tara," as in Gone with the Wind. I'm starting to rehearse again to stay in shape and keep my "show on the road," as they say in show biz jargon. I've often thought life is like a voyage on a ship and each person is the captain of his own soul. Your ship can lead to many adventures, some good, some bad, but the main thing is to keep your ship from crashing into the rocks, by using power of mind. I believe in destiny and in karma, but I also believe that if you sit still and listen, you can hear God. I've worked long and hard in this lifetime, and, if I had it to do all over again, I would probably do it the same way.

"OK, let's go shopping, Deb. I need some new clothes for the tour!"

"What tour?" she asked. I looked at her blankly and said, "I don't know, I've been told psychically I will be going on a tour and must get all my clothes and fittings over with now as there will be no time later this year." She looked exasperated and said, "Here we go again!"

Then came the call. It was Miss Kris Larson from the MGM Studio Video Department inviting me to come to Las Vegas to make a one-hour appearance at the MGM booth for the national video convention, and to meet Ted Turner, the Atlanta TV tycoon. Over 13,000 dealers were expected. "You will only appear for one hour and sign autograph pictures, then be our guest at the Vegas Hilton for three nights. Then we want to talk to you about our MGM video "tour" around the United States. Some of the musicals you made at MGM will be released in an MGM package, and we are sending three or four stars out at different times. Can you go?" I told her I would be thrilled to go. Of course, they would also pay me a handsome salary. I hung up and said, "Deb, the `tour' is on!"

A week later I went over and had lunch with Kris Larson and George Feltenstein. George is a young executive who adores all the MGM films and is a great film historian. He has spent hours working on the videos to bring the color up, and to restore the prints to their original quality. We went for lunch at the old MGM studio, now called Lorimar Productions. We went into the studio commissary and sat in an area that used to be L.B. Mayer's private dining room. The big MGM lion logo sign that had been on top of the old MGM studio has been removed and put on top of the brand new MGM building across the street. Sitting there at lunch, I was ill at ease. I was trying to make conversation with Kris and George, but all I could sense were the ghosts of L.B. Mayer, Clark Gable, Spencer Tracy, and Judy Garland all hovering around me. But, you can't stop progress; for better or for worse, it still goes on.

Yes, I will do the tour and be well paid, of course, but, as the world knows, none of the stars received any residuals from these wonderful old films. We all signed our rights away years ago. The tycoons, like Ted Turner and Kirk Kerkorian, are making millions from them.

Kris suggested that we walk across the street from the Lorimar Studio to the new MGM building so I could see the big lobby. As I walked into this glamorous building, I saw two restaurants, a big projection room, and a small MGM shop. Kris, George and I walked into the shop. It was filled with items of clothing and smaller objects like watches, all with the MGM lion logo on them. I admired a black satin jacket and a watch with the logo and much to my amazement,

Kris and George insisted on buying them both for me as a memory of my visit. I thanked them profusely and said good bye. As I walked to my car I couldn't help thinking how sad I felt. Looking at my watch, I remembered the big lion that roared before each film, and dear MGM, the most powerful studio on earth. It had more stars than there are in the heavens and all that's left for a memory, other than the videos, is a satin jacket and a watch.

How lucky I am to have had a film career in the Golden Era of Hollywood. To have seen the greatest stars and greatest studios and writers; to have known powerful men like L.B. Mayer and Harry Cohn; to have seen the best set designers and song writers as well as costume designers and choreographers at work.

When Lucille Ball died, I was heartbroken, because, without her, my Hollywood career might never have taken place. She discovered me. After her death, they sent a TV truck to Sedona to tape a three-way conversation with the interviewer in New York, Gale Gordon, Lucy's sidekick in her early series, who spoke from California, while I responded from Arizona. The interview and Lucy's death made me think how strange life is. Without me, she might not have met Desi Arnaz, since I introduced them at RKO, while filming "Too Many Girls." We were all so young and happy and my ship of life was loaded down with joy. How many fourteen-year-old girls would ever have had a chance to work in a film like "Stage Door," with the fabulous Katherine Hepburn, and my idol, Ginger Rogers, and to have sung and danced with her? How many people have had directors like Greg Lacava and Frank Capra at the helm of a picture? How lucky could I get?

Sure, I did miss part of my childhood, like riding bikes and playing hopscotch and chewing bubble gum. But I adored every precious moment of my Hollywood career and hope to continue to do so. I lived to see my name up in lights on a sign one block long on Broadway, in "Mame." Then nine years later, my name was up in lights again when "Sugar Babies" played at the Mark Hellinger Theatre in New York.

One "wit" said, "Ann Miller is Hollywood's last standing monument." And you know what? If that's true, I'm proud as hell that I am. For a long-legged gal from Texas, who could not read a note of music, but could tell a conductor what note I felt was wrong; such knowledge had to have come from another lifetime. It is known that Cole Porter could not play a note of music on the piano and Irving Berlin only played with one finger in the key of F. It has to be "far memory."

I am not a teacher but I hope this book will open a door to the psychic world for many people. It is not unusual to have one or more psychic experiences in a lifetime, but most people don't want to discuss them for fear of being thought "odd." This book was written to make you more comfortable with psychic reality and to help you begin "tapping into the force."

Many people walk up to me and thank me for all the years of entertainment I have given them. This always makes me think of a poem by Edwin Markham, an American poet:

THERE IS A DESTINY THAT MAKES US BROTHERS;
NONE GOES HIS WAY ALONE;
ALL THAT WE SEND INTO THE LIVES OF OTHERS
COMES BACK INTO OUR OWN.